First published in Great Britain
by Simon & Schuster UK Ltd, 2013
A CBS Company

Recipes originally published in
Celebration Cupcakes (2011),
Vintage Teatime (2012) and
Chocolate Success (2011)

Simon & Schuster Illustrated Books
Simon & Schuster UK Ltd
222 Gray's Inn Road
London WC1X 8HB
www.simonandschuster.co.uk

Simon & Schuster Australia, Sydney
Simon & Schuster India, New Delhi

10 9 8 7 6 5 4 3 2 1

Design: **Fiona Andreanelli, Richard Proctor**
Food Photography: **Lis Parsons, William Shaw**
Stylist: **Tony Hutchinson**
Home Economy: **Kim Morphew, Sara Lewis**
Recipe Consultant (*Vintage Teatime*): **Sîan Cook**

Colour reproduction by **Dot Gradations Ltd, UK**
Printed and bound in China

A CIP catalogue record for this book is available
from the British Library

ISBN 978-1-4711-3255-1

Notes on the recipes

Both metric and imperial measurements have been given in all recipes. Use one set of measurements only and not a mixture of both. Spoon measures are level and 1 tablespoon = 15 ml, 1 teaspoon = 5 ml.

Preheat ovens before use and cook on the centre shelf unless cooking more than one item. If using a fan oven, reduce the heat by 10–20°C, but check with your handbook. Ovens vary considerably, so get to know your own and adjust accordingly. Check cakes by opening the door a fraction, and turn tins if cakes seem to be browning on one side. Look at cakes 5–10 minutes before the end of cooking and test if needs be. If not quite done by the end of the cooking time, cook a little longer.

Medium eggs have been used unless otherwise stated. This book contains some recipes made with raw or lightly cooked eggs. Pregnant or breast-feeding women, invalids, the elderly and very young children should avoid these dishes. Once prepared, keep refrigerated.

This book contains recipes made with nuts. Those with known allergic reactions to nuts and nut derivatives, pregnant and breast-feeding women and very young children should avoid these dishes.

Note on *Vintage Teatime*: This classic collection of authentic recipes is taken from the WI archives. Recipes date back to 1930 and highlight the wealth of domestic knowledge from individual WI members. With thanks to those who gave advice and support in the research of the book.

The Women's Institute

the**WI**
INSPIRING WOMEN

teatime
collection

**SIMON &
SCHUSTER**
ILLUSTRATED

London · New York · Sydney · Toronto · New Delhi

A CBS COMPANY

Contents

Celebration Cupcakes

Basic cupcakes

Rich chocolate cupcakes

Makes 12
Preparation time: 15 minutes + cooling
Cooking time: 18–20 minutes

75 g (2¾ oz) **unsalted butter**, softened
150 g (5½ oz) **caster sugar**
2 **eggs**
50 g (1¾ oz) **self-raising flour**
100 g (3½ oz) **plain flour**
½ teaspoon **bicarbonate of soda**
40 g (1½ oz) **cocoa powder**, sieved
150 ml (5½ fl oz) **buttermilk**

Preheat the oven to 180°C/350°F/Gas Mark 4. Line a 12-hole muffin tin with paper muffin cases.

Whisk the butter and sugar together using an electric hand whisk or beat with a wooden spoon until pale and creamy. Gradually whisk in the eggs until just combined. Then add both flours, the bicarbonate of soda, cocoa powder and buttermilk, whisking until combined and fluffy.

Divide equally between the paper cases, filling them about two-thirds full, and bake in the oven for 18–20 minutes until golden and risen. Leave to cool in the tin for 5 minutes, then transfer to a wire rack to go cold.

Variations
Chocolate chip: Stir through 50 g (1¾ oz) of white, dark or milk chocolate chips after adding the flour.

Mocha: Stir through 1 tablespoon of instant coffee granules, dissolved in 1 tablespoon of boiling water, along with the buttermilk.

Zesty lemon cupcakes

Makes 12
Preparation time: 15 minutes + cooling
Cooking time: 18–20 minutes

175 g (6 oz) **unsalted butter**, softened
175 g (6 oz) **caster sugar**
3 **eggs**
175 g (6 oz) **self-raising flour**, sieved
zest of 1 large **lemon**
½ teaspoon **baking powder**
2 tablespoons **milk**

Preheat the oven to 190°C/375°F/Gas Mark 5. Line a 12-hole muffin tin with paper muffin cases.

Whisk the butter and sugar together using an electric hand whisk or beat with a wooden spoon until pale and creamy. Gradually whisk in the eggs until just combined. Then add the flour, lemon zest, baking powder and milk. Whisk until combined and fluffy.

Divide equally between the paper cases, filling them about two-thirds full, and bake in the oven for 18–20 minutes until golden and risen. Leave to cool in the tin for 5 minutes, then transfer to a wire rack to go cold.

Variations
Zesty orange: Replace the lemon zest with the grated zest of 1 orange.

Lime and coconut: Replace the lemon zest with the grated zest of 1 lime and add 25 g (1 oz) of desiccated coconut along with the flour.

Poppy seed: Use either orange or lemon zest and add 1 tablespoon of poppy seeds.

Truly vanilla cupcakes

Makes 12
Preparation time: 15 minutes + cooling
Cooking time: 18–20 minutes

125 g (4½ oz) **unsalted butter**, softened
175 g (6 oz) **caster sugar**
1 **vanilla pod**, cut in half and seeds scraped out or
    1 tablespoon **vanilla extract**
3 **eggs**
125 g (4½ oz) **self-raising flour**, sieved
50 g (1¾ oz) '00' grade **plain flour**, sieved
75 ml (3 fl oz) **buttermilk**

Preheat the oven to 190°C/375°F/Gas Mark 5. Line a 12-hole muffin tin with paper muffin cases.

Whisk the butter, sugar and vanilla seeds together using an electric hand whisk or beat with a wooden spoon until pale and creamy. Add the eggs, flours and buttermilk and whisk until combined and fluffy.

Divide equally between the paper cases, filling them about two-thirds full, and bake in the oven for 18–20 minutes until golden and risen. Leave to cool in the tin for 5 minutes, then transfer to a wire rack to go cold.

Variations

Marbled chocolate: At the end of step 2 put half the mixture into another bowl. Stir in 2 tablespoons of sieved cocoa powder. Return the cocoa mixture to the vanilla mixture and gently fold once or twice to marble together. Finish as step 3.

Raspberry swirl: Mash 100 g (3½ oz) of fresh raspberries in a bowl until you have a rough purée. At the end of step 2, fold through the purée until just mixed and slightly marbled. Continue as above.

White chocolate chip: Stir through 50 g (1¾ oz) of white chocolate chips at the end of step 2.

Carrot cupcakes

Makes 12
Preparation time: 20 minutes + cooling
Cooking time: 20 minutes

150 g (5½ oz) **carrots**, peeled
50 g (1¾ oz) **raisins** or **sultanas**
200 g (7 oz) **self-raising flour**, sieved
½ teaspoon **bicarbonate of soda**
150 g (5½ oz) **light muscovado sugar**
zest of 1 **orange**
½ teaspoon **ground mixed spice**
3 **eggs**
100 ml (3½ fl oz) **sunflower oil**
75 ml (3 fl oz) **buttermilk**

Preheat the oven to 190°C/375°F/Gas Mark 5. Line a 12-hole muffin tin with paper muffin cases.

Coarsely grate the carrots into a large bowl. Add the raisins, flour, bicarbonate of soda, sugar, orange zest and mixed spice. Lightly beat together the eggs, oil and buttermilk in a jug until combined. Pour the egg mixture into the flour and stir with a spatula until just combined.

Divide equally between the paper cases and bake in the oven for 20 minutes until lightly golden and risen. Leave to cool in the tin for 5 minutes, then transfer to a wire rack to go cold.

Variations

Courgette and chocolate: Replace the carrots with 150 g (5½ oz) of grated courgettes and use 175 g (6 oz) of self-raising flour, adding 25 g (1 oz) of sieved cocoa powder to the flour. Omit the raisins and orange zest.

Beetroot and cranberry: Replace the carrots with 150 g (5½ oz) of peeled, raw, grated beetroot and replace the raisins with 50 g (1¾ oz) of dried cranberries. Omit the mixed spice.

Coffee and almond cupcakes

Makes 12
Preparation time: 15 minutes + cooling
Cooking time: 20–25 minutes

2 tablespoons instant **coffee** granules
50 ml (2 fl oz) warm **milk**
175 g (6 oz) **unsalted butter**, softened
150 g (5½ oz) **self-raising flour**, sieved
175 g (6 oz) **light brown soft sugar**
3 **eggs**
½ teaspoon **baking powder**
100 g (3½ oz) **ground almonds**

Preheat the oven to 190°C/375°F/Gas Mark 5. Line a 12-hole muffin tin with paper muffin cases.

Dissolve the coffee granules in the warm milk. Put the butter, flour, sugar, eggs, baking powder and ground almonds in a large bowl. Add the coffee milk and whisk together using an electric hand whisk or beat with a wooden spoon until pale and creamy.

Divide equally between the paper cases and bake in the oven for 20–25 minutes until golden and risen. Leave to cool in the tin for 5 minutes, then transfer to a wire rack to go cold.

Variations
Totally almond: Replace the coffee granules with 1 teaspoon of almond extract. There is no need to warm the milk. Just add with all the other ingredients.

Totally nuts: Omit the coffee granules, simply whizz 100 g (3½ oz) of walnuts, pecans or hazelnuts and use them instead of the ground almonds.

Gorgeous ginger cupcakes

Makes 12
Preparation time: 20 minutes + cooling
Cooking time: 18–20 minutes

200 g (7 oz) **unsalted butter**
75 g (2¾ oz) **dark muscovado sugar**
100 g (3½ oz) **golden syrup**
175 g (6 oz) **self-raising flour**
¼ teaspoon **bicarbonate of soda**
2 teaspoons **ground ginger**
30 g (1¼ oz) **glacé ginger**, finely chopped
3 **eggs**, beaten

Preheat the oven to 190°C/375°F/Gas Mark 5. Line a 12-hole muffin tin with paper muffin cases.

Put the butter, sugar and golden syrup into a large bowl and beat together until smooth and creamy. Add the flour, bicarbonate of soda, ground ginger, glacé ginger and eggs and whisk with an electric hand whisk or beat with a wooden spoon until combined.

Divide equally between the paper cases and bake in the oven for 18–20 minutes until golden and risen. Leave to cool in the tin for 5 minutes, then transfer to a wire rack to go cold.

Variations
Golden syrup: Use 75 g (2¾ oz) of light brown soft sugar instead of the dark muscovado and omit the ground and glacé ginger.

Spiced cupcakes: Replace the ground ginger with 2 teaspoons of ground mixed spice, and the glacé ginger with 30 g (1¼ oz) of finely chopped candied peel.

Basic cupcake frostings

Buttercream

To ice 12 cupcakes
Preparation time: 10 minutes

125 g (4½ oz) **unsalted butter**, softened
250 g (9 oz) **icing sugar**, sieved
2 tablespoons **boiled water**, cooled

Whisk the butter in a bowl until fluffy. Gradually add the icing sugar and whisk until it comes together. Add the water and whisk until light and fluffy. Use as required.

Variations
Replace the water with the following:

Lemon – use the juice of 1 large lemon

Orange – use the juice of ½ an orange

Vanilla – use 2 teaspoons of vanilla extract

Coffee – dissolve 1 tablespoon of instant coffee granules in 2 tablespoons of boiling water

Chocolate – mix 2 tablespoons of cocoa powder with 2 tablespoons of boiling water

Cream cheese frosting

To ice 12 cupcakes
Preparation time: 10 minutes

200 g (7 oz) **icing sugar**, sieved
150 g (5½ oz) **full fat cream cheese**
50 g (1¾ oz) **Quark**
50 g (1¾ oz) **unsalted butter**, softened

In a bowl, mix together the icing sugar, cream cheese, Quark and butter until you have a smooth icing. Use as required.

Variations
Lemon or Lime: Add the grated zest of 1 lemon or lime.

Orange: Add the grated zest of ½ an orange.

Vanilla: Add the seeds from ½ a vanilla pod.

Marshmallow icing

To ice 12 cupcakes
Preparation time: 15 minutes + cooling

1 large **egg white**
a pinch of **cream of tartar**
60 g (2 oz) **caster sugar**
75 g (2¾ oz) **mini white marshmallows**

Put the egg white and cream of tartar in a heatproof bowl. Whisk until soft peaks form using an electric hand whisk. Then gradually whisk in the sugar until you have a glossy meringue and the sugar has dissolved.

Put the bowl over a pan of simmering water and add the marshmallows. Whisk continuously for about 5 minutes until the marshmallows have nearly melted.

Remove from the heat and whisk for a further 5 minutes until the marshmallows have completely melted and the mixture thickens sufficiently. Leave to cool for 15 minutes, stirring occasionally until the mixture stands in soft peaks. Use as required.

Glacé icing

To ice 12 cupcakes
Preparation time: 5 minutes

300 g (10½ oz) **icing sugar**, sieved
2 teaspoons **unsalted butter**, melted
1–2 tablespoons **boiled water**, cooled

Put the icing sugar and butter in a bowl and gradually stir in the water until you get a smooth, thick icing. Use as required.

Variations

Chocolate glacé icing: Omit the water. In a small pan gradually mix 100 ml (3½ fl oz) of milk into 50 g (1¾ oz) of cocoa powder until smooth. Gently heat until hot. Then stir into the icing sugar and butter.

Passion fruit icing: Replace the water with the sieved juice from 1–2 ripe passion fruit.

Coffee icing: Dissolve 1 tablespoon of instant coffee granules in the boiling water. Allow to cool before using.

Lemon icing: Use the juice of ½ a lemon instead of the water.

Royal icing

To ice 12 cupcakes
Preparation time: 5 minutes

5 tablespoons **cold water**
500 g (1 lb 2 oz) **royal icing sugar**

Put the water into a bowl and add the icing sugar. Whisk for
5 minutes using an electric hand whisk until you get firm peaks.
Use as required.

Chocolate ganache

To ice 12 cupcakes
Preparation time: 15 minutes

75 ml (3 fl oz) **double cream**
25 g (1 oz) **unsalted butter**
200 g (7 oz) **dark chocolate**, finely chopped
100 g (3½ oz) **white chocolate**, finely chopped

Put the cream, butter and both chocolates in a heatproof bowl
and place over a pan of barely simmering water. Gently heat
until the chocolate and butter have melted, stirring occasionally.
Remove from the heat and use as required.

Variation
White chocolate ganache: Omit the dark chocolate and use
300 g (10½ oz) of white chocolate.

Runny fondant icing

To ice 12 cupcakes
Preparation time: 5 minutes

300 g (10½ oz) fondant **icing sugar**, sieved
approx. 3 tablespoons **cold water**

Put the icing sugar in a bowl and gradually stir in the water until
you get a smooth thick icing. Use as required.

Variation
If you want, why not flavour royal icing or runny fondant icing by
using 4 tablespoons of fruit juice instead of the water.

Birthday balloon cupcakes

You can use any sweets you like, just as long as they look like balloons.

Makes 12
Decorating time:
  20 minutes

52.5 g packet **fruit pastilles**
2 **strawberry laces**
1 quantity **Lemon glacé
  icing** (see variation,
  page 12)
12 **Zesty lemon cupcakes**
  (see page 6)

Carefully cut each fruit pastille in half horizontally using a sharp knife, and cut the strawberry laces into short lengths.

Using a small palette knife, spread the glace icing all over the top of the cakes, smoothing it down as you go. Let the icing settle for a few minutes.

Decorate each cupcake with two or three fruit pastilles and arrange a strawberry lace per fruit pastille to look like a balloon. Leave to set.

Tips Most supermarkets have their own range of 'retro' style sweets like strawberry laces, but if not then any good local newsagent should stock them. To finish the look, use 'happy birthday' style candles.

Orange or lime glacé icing also works well with these cupcakes, just replace the lemon juice in the icing with the same quantity of orange or lime juice.

Little pirate cupcakes

Every little boy dreams of being a pirate so why not make him the captain and his birthday cake the crew!

Makes 12
Decorating time:
  45 minutes

300 g (10½ oz) **ready-to-roll white fondant icing**
12 **Zesty lemon cupcakes** (see page 6)
50 g (1¾ oz) **apricot jam,** melted
75 g (2¾ oz) **ready-to-roll black fondant icing**
boiled water, cooled
75 g (2¾ oz) **ready-to-roll red fondant icing**
50 g (1¾ oz) **butter,** softened
100 g (3½ oz) **icing sugar,** sieved, plus extra for dusting
black food colouring

Equipment
6.5 cm (2½ inch) round cutter
6 cm (2¼ inch) round cutter
disposable piping bags
plain writing nozzle

Lightly dust a clean work surface with a little icing sugar. Roll out the white fondant icing until about 3–4 mm (⅛–¼ inch) thick. Using a 6.5 cm (2½ inch) round cookie cutter, stamp out 12 circles. You may need to re-roll the icing.

Brush the tops of the cupcakes with the apricot jam then put a white circle on to the top of each cupcake, lightly pressing down.

Roll out the black fondant icing until about 3–4 mm (⅛–¼ inch) thick and stamp out three circles using a 6 cm (2¼ inch) round cookie cutter. Cut each circle in half to make six semi-circles. Lightly brush the underside of each semi-circle with cooled boiled water and place on the top half of six cupcakes to look like a hat. Using the trimmings, cut out 12 very small triangles and arrange to one side of the semi-circles to look like ties. Repeat with the red fondant icing and the remaining cupcakes.

Put the butter into a bowl and whisk until fluffy. Gradually add the icing sugar and about 1–2 teaspoons of cooled boiled water and whisk until light and fluffy. Put half the buttercream into a piping bag with a writing nozzle and pipe small dots over the red hats and skull and crossbones over the black hats.

Squeeze any excess buttercream back into the bowl and wash out the nozzle. Colour the remaining buttercream black, put into a piping bag with the writing nozzle and pipe an eye patch, an eye and a mouth over each pirate.

Little princess cupcakes

Perfect for any little girl's birthday. If you like you can use non-edible butterfly cake toppers.

Makes 12
Decorating time:
  30 minutes

1 quantity **Lemon buttercream** (see variation, page 10)
red food colouring
blue food colouring
green food colouring
12 **Zesty lemon cupcakes** (see page 6)
12 ready-made **edible wafer daisies**
6 ready-made **sugar butterfly decorations**

Equipment
disposable piping bag
small star nozzle

Divide the buttercream in half and put in separate bowls. Colour one half pink using a few drops of red food colouring and beating with a spatula until the right shade. Colour the remaining buttercream using the blue and green food colouring until you get a turquoise colour, beating again with a spatula.

Spread a little of the pink buttercream over the tops of six cupcakes using a small palette knife. Repeat with the turquoise buttercream and the remaining six cupcakes.

Put the pink buttercream into a piping bag with a small star nozzle and pipe a star border around the edge of each pink cupcake. Repeat with the turquoise buttercream. Decorate each cupcake with a wafer daisy and then choose six to have butterflies as well.

Birthday present cupcakes

Look out for multicoloured fizzy belt sweets in newsagents or sweet shops, or use anything similar that can be bent.

Makes 12
Decorating time:
  30 minutes + 1 hour
  setting

12 **multicoloured fizzy belt**
  sweets (approx 25 x 2 cm
  /10 x ¾ inch)
1 quantity **Marshmallow**
  icing (see page 12)
12 **Carrot cupcakes** (see
  page 7)
edible pastel pink glitter

Equipment
disposable piping bag
large star nozzle

Cut six sweets in half. Cut a further two sweets in half lengthways, then cut each thin length into three short lengths. To make a bow, take a sweet half and fold in half, but so the join is in the middle. Take a short length and wrap it around the join a few times, quite tightly. Repeat to make 12 bows.

To make ribbon tails, cut each of the remaining four sweets in half lengthways, then cut each of these in to three to make 24 short thin strips. Cut a small triangle out of one end of a strip, to give you a fork like the tail of a ribbon. Repeat with the remaining strips.

Put the marshmallow icing into a piping bag with a large star nozzle and pipe zigzag patterns or large swirls over the top of each cupcake, starting from the outside edge and working your way to the centre.

Put two thin ribbon tails on top of each cupcake, then top each with a bow. Sprinkle with a little glitter and leave to set for 1 hour.

Tip If you like, you could make the ribbon bows out of coloured, ready-to-roll fondant icing instead.

Dotty name cupcakes

Chocolate beans are a great and easy way to decorate cakes. You can also use mini Smarties or small dragées instead.

Makes 12
Preparation and decorating time:
  30 minutes + cooling
Cooking time:
  20 minutes

Cinnamon cupcakes
125 ml (4 fl oz) **Guinness**
150 g (5½ oz) **dark brown soft sugar**
150 g (5½ oz) **unsalted butter**, melted
¼ teaspoon **bicarbonate of soda**
225 g (8 oz) **self-raising flour**
2 teaspoons **ground cinnamon**
3 **eggs**, beaten

To decorate
1 quantity **Buttercream** (see page 10)
edible cream glitter
chocolate beans or **mini Smarties**

Preheat the oven to 180°C/350°F/Gas Mark 4. Line a 12-hole muffin tin with paper muffin cases.

Put the Guinness, sugar and butter in a small pan and gently heat until combined. Stir in the bicarbonate of soda and leave to cool.

Meanwhile put the flour and cinnamon in a bowl. Add the eggs and stir with a spatula until combined. Gradually stir in the cooked Guinness mixture until combined, beating well between each addition.

Transfer to a jug and divide between the paper cases. Bake in the oven for 20 minutes until golden and risen. Leave to cool in the tin for 5 minutes, then transfer to a wire rack to go cold.

Using a small palette knife, spread the buttercream over the tops of the cupcakes until covered. Sprinkle the tops of the cakes with a little edible glitter. Using the chocolate beans, spell out 'Happy Birthday' or the name of the person with a birthday, using each cupcake as one or two letters.

Tip You may wish to make double the batch so that you can spell out 'Happy Birthday' and the person's name.

Sparkly star cupcakes

This works well with other shapes too. Just choose your favourite cookie cutter or pipe freehand designs.

Makes 12
Decorating time:
30 minutes

300 g (10½ oz) **ready-to-roll white fondant icing**

50 g (1¾ oz) **apricot jam**, melted

12 **Carrot cupcakes** (see page 7)

50 g (1¾ oz) **unsalted butter**, softened

100 g (3½ oz) **icing sugar**, sieved, plus extra for dusting

1–2 teaspoons **boiled water**, cooled

hundreds and thousands

Equipment
6.5 cm (2½ inch) round cutter
disposable piping bag
plain writing nozzle
star cookie cutter

Lightly dust a clean work surface with a little icing sugar. Roll out the fondant icing until about 3–4 mm (⅛–¼ inch) thick. Then, using a 6.5 cm (2½ inch) round cookie cutter, stamp out 12 circles. You may need to re-roll the icing. Brush the tops of the cupcakes with the apricot jam then put a white circle on to the top of each cupcake, lightly pressing down.

Put the butter into a bowl and whisk until fluffy. Gradually add the icing sugar and water and whisk until light and fluffy. Put the buttercream into a piping bag with a plain writing nozzle.

Press a small star cookie cutter into the top of each cupcake to score the star shape into the icing. Using this as a guide, pipe around the edge of the star and then fill in with buttercream.

Sprinkle the stars all over with hundred and thousands, shaking off any excess.

Black Forest cupcakes

Store in an airtight container in the fridge for up to 3 days. For adults, why not add a splash of cassis to the whipped cream?

Makes 12
Decorating time:
  20 minutes

12 **Rich chocolate cupcakes** (see page 6)
75 g (2¾ oz) **black cherry jam**
200 ml (7 fl oz) **double cream**
3–4 tablespoons **icing sugar**, sieved
100 g (3½ oz) **flaked almonds**, toasted
12 whole fresh **cherries**

Using a small serrated knife, cut a cone shape from the top of each cupcake. Put a little cherry jam into the hole in each cake and replace the cones.

Whisk the cream with an electric hand whisk until soft peaks form. Stir through the icing sugar to taste.

Reserve about 4 tablespoons of cream. Using a small palette knife, spread the remaining cream over the tops of the cupcakes until covered. Scatter with the flaked almonds, ensuring an even covering.

Put a small dollop of the reserved cream on top of each cupcake and top each with a fresh cherry. Chill in the fridge until required.

Tip If fresh cherries are out of season, then use frozen stoned cherries. Simply defrost, then pat dry on kitchen towel before using to decorate the cakes.

Pure white cupcakes

These make the perfect cake for a christening celebration. The white doves are available from most good cake shops.

Makes 12
Decorating time:
  30 minutes + setting

150 g (5½ oz) **icing sugar**, sieved, plus extra for dusting

1 teaspoon **unsalted butter**, melted

2–3 tablespoons **boiled water**, cooled

75 g (2¾ oz) **desiccated coconut**

12 **Lime and coconut cupcakes** (see variation, page 6)

100 g (3½ oz) **ready-to-roll white fondant icing**

white mimosa balls

6 **white plastic doves** (optional)

edible cream or lemon glitter

Equipment
flower cutters

Put the icing sugar and butter into a bowl and stir in the water until you get a smooth, thick, but runny, icing. Put the coconut into another bowl. Dip the top of each cupcake into the icing, allow the excess to drip off and then dip into the coconut, gently pressing down until the top of the cupcake is coated.

Lightly dust a clean work surface with a little icing sugar. Roll out the fondant icing until about 3–4 mm (⅛–¼ inch) thick. Cut out a range of large and small flowers using a flower cutter. Press a mimosa ball into the centre of each flower.

Using the leftover runny icing, dab a small amount on to the base of each flower and stick the flowers to the top of the cupcakes. Do the same with the white doves (if using). Sprinkle with a little glitter and leave to set.

New baby cupcakes

Depending on whether the new arrival is a girl or a boy, choose decorations in pink or blue.

Makes 12
Preparation time:
  30 minutes

1 quantity **Lemon buttercream** (see variation, page 10)
12 **Zesty lemon cupcakes** (see page 6)
6 ready-made **blue** or **pink feet sugar decorations**
9 ready-made **blue** or **pink baby sugar decorations**
edible silver balls
edible cream or lemon glitter

Equipment
disposable piping bag
small star nozzle

Spread a little of the buttercream over the tops of six cupcakes using a small palette knife.

Put the remaining buttercream into a piping bag with a small star nozzle and pipe a star border around the edge of the six iced cupcakes. Decorate the remaining cupcakes with small rosettes, starting on the outside edge and working your way into the centre to cover the tops.

Decorate each cupcake with a baby decoration or pair of feet. Sprinkle the piped cupcakes with silver balls and all the cakes a dusting of glitter.

Heart cupcakes

For those romantic moments, these cakes will soon melt any heart.

Makes 12
Decorating time:
** 30 minutes**

1 tablespoon **rose water**
red food colouring
1 quantity **Buttercream** (see page 10)
12 **Zesty lemon cupcakes** (see page 6)
icing sugar, for dusting
75 g (2¾ oz) **ready-to-roll red fondant icing**
red, **heart-shaped sugar sprinkles**
edible red glitter

Equipment
disposable piping bag
large star nozzle
heart-shaped cutter

Mix the rose water and a little red food colouring into the buttercream until the buttercream is pink in colour. Put into a piping bag with a large star nozzle.

Pipe stars over the top of six cupcakes, starting on the outside edge and working your way into the centre to cover the tops. Pipe a big swirl on to the top of the remaining cupcakes, starting on the outside and working your way to the centre.

Lightly dust a clean work surface with icing sugar and roll the fondant icing out until about 3–4 mm (⅛–¼ inch) thick. Using a heart-shaped cookie cutter, stamp out six large hearts.

Decorate the cupcakes with the piped stars with a fondant heart, and scatter the remaining cupcakes with heart-shaped sprinkles. Lightly dust all the cupcakes with a little glitter.

St Patrick's Day cupcakes

With the luck of the Irish, spread the joy with these leprechaun-inspired cakes.

Makes 12
Decorating time:
30 minutes + 1 hour setting

1 quantity **Buttercream** (see page 10)
green food colouring
12 **Cinnamon cupcakes** (see Dotty name cupcakes, page 22)
4 teaspoons **cold water**
150 g (5½ oz) **royal icing sugar**, sieved
edible silver balls
edible green glitter

Equipment
disposable piping bags
small star nozzle
large petal nozzle

Divide the buttercream in half. Colour one half green using a few drops of green food colouring and beating with a spatula until you get the right shade. Using a small palette knife, spread the green buttercream over the tops of six cupcakes until covered. Cover the remaining cupcakes with the plain buttercream.

Whisk the cold water and icing sugar for a few minutes until stiff peaks form. If it is a little too stiff, add a drop more water. Divide in half. Colour one half green using a few drops of green food colouring and beating with a spatula until you get the right shade.

Put the white icing into a piping bag with a small star nozzle and pipe small stars around the edge of the six cupcakes covered with green buttercream. Put a silver ball on top of each star.

Put the green icing into a piping bag with a large petal nozzle and pipe shamrock petals on top of the remaining cupcakes. Put the leftover icing into another disposable piping bag and snip off the end. Pipe a small stalk on each shamrock. Sprinkle all the cupcakes with glitter and leave to set for 1 hour.

Valentine's Day cupcakes

Let these cupcakes speak from your heart. Be as creative as you like and say as little or as much as you desire.

Makes 12
Preparation and decorating time:
 45 minutes + 1 hour setting + cooling
Cooking time:
 18–20 minutes

Turkish delight cupcakes
175 g (6 oz) **unsalted butter**, softened
100 g (3½ oz) **caster sugar**
3 **eggs**
175 g (6 oz) **self-raising flour**, sieved
½ teaspoon **baking powder**
1 tablespoon **rose water**
100 g (3½ oz) **rose Turkish delight**, finely diced

To decorate
25 g (1 oz) **unsalted butter**, softened
50 g (1¾ oz) **icing sugar**
1–2 teaspoons **boiled water**, cooled
1 quantity **Chocolate ganache** (see page 13)

Equipment
disposable piping bag
plain writing nozzle

Preheat the oven to 190°C/375°F/Gas Mark 5. Line a 12-hole muffin tin with paper muffin cases.

Whisk the butter and sugar together with an electric hand whisk or beat with a wooden spoon until pale and creamy. Gradually whisk in the eggs until just combined, then add the flour, baking powder and rose water and whisk until combined and fluffy. Fold through the Turkish delight.

Divide the mixture evenly between the paper cases and bake in the oven for 18–20 minutes until golden and risen. Leave to cool in the tin for 5 minutes, then transfer to a wire rack to go cold.

To decorate, whisk the butter until fluffy then gradually sieve in the icing sugar and whisk until it comes together. Add the water and whisk again until light and fluffy.

Using a small palette knife, spread a little of the chocolate ganache over the tops of the cupcakes to cover. Leave to set for 30 minutes.

Put the buttercream into a piping bag with a writing nozzle. Pipe words such as 'I Love You' or 'Be Mine', dots, kisses and heart shapes over the top of the cakes. Leave to set.

Variation
Replace the rose Turkish delight with lemon Turkish delight and use 1 tablespoon of lemon juice instead of the rose water.

Mother's Day cupcakes

Say it with flowers this Mother's Day, but instead of a bunch of flowers why not give a bunch of cakes.

Makes 12
Decorating time:
 30 minutes

1 quantity **Orange buttercream** (see variation, page 10)
pink food colouring
12 **Zesty orange cupcakes** (see variation, page 6)
12 ready-made **edible large pink flowers**

Equipment
disposable piping bags
large star nozzle
large writing nozzle

Put 3 tablespoons of buttercream into a bowl and mix in a little pink food colouring until light pink in colour.

Using a small palette knife, spread a little of the uncoloured buttercream over the tops of six cupcakes until covered. Put the remaining buttercream into a piping bag with a large star nozzle and pipe a big swirl on to the top of the remaining cupcakes, starting on the outside and working your way to the centre.

Put the pink buttercream into a piping bag with a large writing nozzle. Pipe polka dots over the top of three flat-iced cupcakes, then pipe dots around the edge of the remaining three flat-iced cupcakes. Decorate all the cupcakes with a large pink flower.

St George's Day cupcakes

Raise the flag on 23rd April with these inspired cakes.

Makes 12
Decorating time:
  30 minutes

icing sugar, for dusting
75 g (2¾ oz) **ready-to-roll white fondant icing**
25 g (1 oz) **ready-to-roll red fondant icing**
blue food colouring
1 quantity **Vanilla buttercream** (see variation, page 10)
12 **Truly vanilla cupcakes** (see page 7)
red and blue sugar sprinkles or **confetti**
edible blue glitter

Equipment
4 cm (1½ inch) round cutter

Lightly dust a clean work surface with icing sugar and roll the white fondant icing out until about 5 mm (¼ inch) thick. Using a 4 cm (1½ inch) round cookie cutter, stamp out 12 circles. You may need to re-roll the icing.

Roll a little of the red fondant icing between your fingers and the work surface to make a thin sausage. Cut in half and lay in a cross over the top of one white circle. Lightly roll with a rolling pin to flatten. Re-stamp out the circle and set aside. Repeat with the remaining red fondant icing and white circles to make 12 round St George's flags.

Mix a little blue food colouring into the buttercream until combined and light blue in colour. Using a small palette knife, spread the buttercream over the tops of the cupcakes to cover.

Put a St George's flag on top of each cupcake, pressing down lightly, and then sprinkle the exposed buttercream with the red and blue sprinkles or confetti and a little blue glitter.

Easter nest cupcakes

During the Easter holidays there are lots of different sweets around, so why not use chocolate bunnies or chicks.

Makes 12
Decorating time:
30 minutes + 1 hour setting

150 g (5½ oz) **dark chocolate**, broken into pieces

1 tablespoon **unsalted butter**, softened

25 ml (1 fl oz) **double cream**

25 g (1 oz) **icing sugar**, sieved

2 teaspoons **boiling water**

4 whole **shredded wheat**, crushed

12 **Rich chocolate cupcakes** (see page 6)

about 36 **chocolate mini eggs**

Put the chocolate, butter and double cream in a heatproof bowl and place over a pan of barely simmering water. Gently heat, stirring occasionally until melted.

Stir in the icing sugar until combined. Then stir in the boiling water until you have a smooth icing.

Add the crushed shredded wheat to the bowl and stir with a spatula until coated in the chocolate.

Put a generous spoonful of the topping on top of each cupcake, making a dent in the middle, to make it look like a nest. Arrange the mini eggs in the centre of each nest and leave to set for 1 hour.

Father's Day cupcakes

Make his day special this year and give him a golf course!

Makes 12
Decorating time:
45 minutes + 1 hour
setting

12 **Lime and coconut**
cupcakes (see variation,
page 6)
75 g (2¾ oz) **unsalted butter**,
softened
300 g (10½ oz) **icing sugar**,
sieved
juice of 1 **lime**
green food colouring
yellow food colouring
yellow coloured sugar or
yellow sugar strands or
sprinkles
non-edible mini golfer
figurines
white mimosa balls
cocktail sticks for flag
poles

Equipment
disposable piping bags
grass nozzle

Arrange the cupcakes on a serving plate. Whisk the butter until fluffy, then gradually add half the icing sugar and half the lime juice, whisking again until light and fluffy.

Divide the buttercream in half. Colour one half grass green using a few drops of green and yellow food colouring and beating with a spatula until you get the right shade. Colour the remainder a sandy yellow using yellow food colouring.

Put the green buttercream into a piping bag with a grass nozzle and pipe grass-like tufts over some of the cupcakes, creating the outside edge of the golf course.

Using a small palette knife, spread the yellow buttercream over some of the tops of the cupcakes to look like bunkers. Sprinkle generously with the yellow sugar or sprinkles.

Put the remaining icing sugar in a bowl and gradually stir in the remaining lime juice until you get a smooth thick icing. If it is too thick, add a drop more water. Colour with green food colouring until you get a grass-like colour. Put in a disposable piping bag, snip off the end and use to cover any remaining cake, so it looks like a fairway. Leave for 15 minutes until nearly set.

When almost set, arrange the mini golfers on top of the cakes, using the mimosa balls as golf balls. Make a small paper flag and attach to a cocktail stick as a flag pole. Leave for 1 hour to set.

Tip If you can't find coloured sugar, put some granulated sugar in a freezer bag with a little edible yellow dust. Shake to colour the sugar.

Halloween cupcakes

This is a great one for children. Be as creative as you like. You could do all monster faces – just colour all the buttercream green.

Makes 12
Decorating time:
  30 minutes

1 quantity **Vanilla buttercream** (see variation, page 10)
green food colouring
black food colouring
12 **Spiced cupcakes** (see variation, page 8)
sweets such as fizzy fangs, liquorice, mini marshmallows, chocolate beans, strawberry pencils and jelly beans
white sugar sprinkles or **strands**
plastic non-edible Halloween cake decorations
edible black glitter

Divide the buttercream in half. Colour one half green using a few drops of green food colouring and beating with a spatula until you get the right shade. Colour the remainder dark grey using the black food colouring.

Using a small palette knife, spread the green buttercream over the tops of six cupcakes until covered. Do the same with the grey buttercream and the remaining cupcakes.

Using the selection of sweets, make monster faces on the green cupcakes. For eyes, use liquorice rolls or cut marshmallows in half and stick brown chocolate beans on top. Finely slice liquorice twists to look like hair, slice strawberry pencils or use red jelly beans to look like teeth.

Sprinkle the grey cupcakes with white sugar sprinkles and top each with a plastic cake decoration and a little black glitter.

Christmas bauble cupcakes

Make these cakes really Christmassy with cranberries. Omit the poppy seeds and use 50 g (1¾ oz) of dried cranberries instead.

Makes 12
Decorating time:
30 minutes + 1 hour setting

icing sugar, for dusting
100 g (3½ oz) **ready-to-roll white fondant icing**
12 **Poppy seed cupcakes** (see variation, page 6)
50 g (1¾ oz) **apricot jam**, melted
100 g (3½ oz) **ready-to-roll red fondant icing**
100 g (3½ oz) **ready-to-roll green fondant icing**
4 teaspoons **cold water**
150 g (5½ oz) **royal icing sugar**, sieved
edible silver and **gold balls**

Equipment
6.5 cm (2½ inch) round cutter
disposable piping bag
plain writing nozzle

Lightly dust a clean work surface with a little icing sugar. Roll out the white fondant icing until about 3–4 mm (⅛–¼ inch) thick. Then, using a 6.5 cm (2½ inch) round cookie cutter, stamp out four circles. You may need to re-roll the icing.

Brush the tops of four cupcakes with the apricot jam then put a white circle on each, lightly pressing down. Repeat with the red and green fondant icing and the remaining cupcakes.

Whisk the cold water and icing sugar together for a few minutes until stiff peaks form. If it is a little too stiff, add a drop more water. Put into a piping bag with a plain writing nozzle.

Pipe a circle around the outside edge of each cupcake and then pipe curved lines, dots, zigzags or stars in the centre of each cupcake to look like a bauble. Decorate with gold or silver balls. Leave to set for 1 hour.

Fruit tart cupcakes

You can top these cupcakes with any fruits you like, such as fresh apricots or figs, or vary them depending on the season.

Makes 12
Preparation and decorating time:
30 minutes + cooling
Cooking time:
15–18 minutes

125 g (4½ oz) **unsalted butter**, softened
125 g (4½ oz) **caster sugar**
2 **eggs**
125 g (4½ oz) **self-raising flour**
2 **kiwi fruit**, peeled and cut into 12 slices
12 **green** or **red seedless grapes**
6 **strawberries**, sliced

Crème patisserie
4 **egg yolks**
60 g (2 oz) **caster sugar**
2 teaspoons **cornflour**
25 g (1 oz) **plain flour**
1 teaspoon **vanilla extract**
300 ml (10 fl oz) **milk**

Preheat the oven to 190°C/375°F/Gas Mark 5. Line a 12-hole muffin tin with paper muffin cases.

Whisk the butter and sugar together with an electric hand whisk or beat with a wooden spoon until pale and creamy. Gradually whisk in the eggs until just combined. Add the self-raising flour and whisk again until combined and fluffy.

Divide between the paper cases and bake in the oven for 15–18 minutes until golden and risen. Leave to cool in the tin for 5 minutes, then transfer to a wire rack to go cold.

Meanwhile, for the crème patisserie, mix together the egg yolks, sugar, cornflour, plain flour and vanilla extract. Put the milk in a small pan and bring just to the boil. Gradually stir into the egg yolk mixture until smooth and combined. Rinse out the pan and return the hot milk mixture. Gently bring to the boil, stirring until thickened. Transfer to a bowl, cover with a damp piece of greaseproof paper and leave to go cold.

When the crème patisserie and cakes are cold, whisk the crème patisserie with a fork to loosen and then spoon a little on to the top of each cupcake, levelling the top with a small palette knife.

Arrange the fruit on top of each cake and serve immediately or store in the fridge until required.

New Year cupcakes

When the clock strikes 12, indulge in a clock-inspired cupcake. Arrange like a clock on a serving platter.

Makes 12
Decorating time:
30 minutes

1 quantity **Coffee buttercream** (see variation, page 10)
12 **Coffee and almond cupcakes** (see page 8)
icing sugar, for dusting
100 g (3½ oz) **ready-to-roll black fondant icing**
edible gold glitter

Equipment
disposable piping bag
large shell nozzle
large number cutters

Put the buttercream into a piping bag with a large shell nozzle and pipe a continuous line all the way around the edge of a cupcake. Then pipe small rosettes all over the centre of the cake until the top of the cake is covered. Repeat with the remaining cupcakes.

Lightly dust a clean work surface with a little icing sugar. Roll out the black fondant icing until about 3–4 mm (⅛–¼ inch) thick. Using large number cookie cutters stamp out the numbers 1 to 12.

Sprinkle the tops of the cupcakes with a little gold glitter. Top each cake with a number from 1–12 and arrange in a circle like a clock.

Tip If you like you could make paper clock hands out of black card and put them in the middle of the arranged cupcakes.

Vintage chic cupcakes

If you wish, keep the cupcakes in their cases and just decorate the tops using 300 g (10½ oz) of ready-to-roll fondant icing.

Makes 12
Decorating time: 1 hour
+ 1 hour setting

900 g (2 lb) **ready-to-roll ivory fondant icing**
pink food colouring
blue food colouring
green food colouring
12 **Zesty lemon cupcakes** (see page 6)
100 g (3½ oz) **apricot jam**, melted
icing sugar, for dusting
boiled water, cooled
150 g (5½ oz) **royal icing sugar**, sieved
4 teaspoons **cold water**
ready-made **sugar flowers**

Equipment
5 cm (2 inch) round cutter
disposable piping bag
plain writing nozzle

Divide the fondant icing into three equal pieces. Wrap each piece in cling film while you work to prevent it from drying out. Colour one piece pale pink using the pink food colouring. Colour a second piece pale turquoise using a little blue and green food colouring.

Take a cupcake out of its paper case and discard the case. Brush the cake all over the top and sides with apricot jam and place on a board.

Lightly dust a clean work surface with a little icing sugar. Roll a quarter of the ivory fondant icing out until about 3 mm (⅛ inch) thick. Cut out a 20 x 4 cm (8 x 1½ inch) rectangle. Wrap the rectangle around the sides of the cupcake, smoothing with your hands to cover the sides of the cake and just overlapping the top.

Reroll the trimmings and stamp out a circle using a 5 cm (2 inch) round cutter. Brush the rim with a little cooled water and place on top of the cake, pressing down gently and reshaping where necessary. Repeat with the remaining cupcakes and icings. You should end up with four ivory, four pink and four turquoise cupcakes.

Whisk the icing sugar and cooled water for a few minutes until stiff peaks form. If it is a little too stiff, add a drop more water. Put the icing into a piping bag with a plain writing nozzle.

Pipe different designs on each cupcake, such as small dots around the edge, lines across the middle or swirls over the top and sides. Finish each with a sugar flower. Arrange on a serving plate and leave to set for 1 hour.

Tips Do not store in an airtight container, as the icing will become sweaty. The cakes will stay fresh for at least 3 days once iced.

To finish the look, why not tie a ribbon around the middle of each cake and secure with a little royal icing.

Spring blossom cupcakes

You can find a range of flower cutters from most good cake shops, including gerberas, daisies and marguerites.

Makes 12
Decorating time:
   30 minutes

1 quantity **Lemon buttercream** (see variation, page 10)
blue food colouring
12 **Raspberry swirl cupcakes** (see variation, page 7)
icing sugar, for dusting
125 g (4½ oz) **ready-to-roll white fondant icing**
edible silver balls

Equipment
flower cutters
disposable piping bag
writing nozzle

Reserve 2 tablespoons of the buttercream. Colour the remaining buttercream with a few drops of blue food colouring, beating with a spatula until light blue. Spread the blue buttercream over the tops of the cupcakes using a small palette knife.

Lightly dust a clean work surface with icing sugar and roll the fondant icing out until about 3–4 mm (⅛–¼ inch) thick. Using a selection of large, medium and small flower cutters, stamp out lots of flowers until the icing has been used up. Arrange a few different sized flowers on top of each cupcake, spacing them so they look like spring blossom.

Put the reserved buttercream into a piping bag with a plain writing nozzle and pipe flower stems joining some of the flowers together and coming from the side of each cake.

Prick a hole in the centre of any large flowers using a skewer. Arrange a silver ball in the centre of each flower.

Tip If making for a wedding, this recipe can easily be doubled depending on how many cupcakes you need. The cupcakes with the blue butter cream on them can also be frozen in advance. Just defrost and decorate with the flowers, stems and silver balls.

Monogram cupcakes

The fondant hearts can be made in advance and stored between baking parchment. Do not store in an airtight container.

Makes 12
Decorating time:
  30 minutes +
  24 hours drying

icing sugar, for dusting
75 g (3¾ oz) **flower paste**
  (see Tip, page 93)
75 g (3¾ oz) **ready-to-roll**
  white fondant icing
1 quantity **Orange**
  buttercream (see
  variation, page 10)
pink food colouring
blue food colouring
12 **Gorgeous ginger**
  cupcakes (see page 8)

Equipment
medium heart cutter
small alphabet cutters
disposable piping bag's
large star nozzle
small writing nozzle

Lightly dust a clean work surface with a little icing sugar. Mix together the flower paste and fondant icing, then roll out until about 3–4 mm (⅛–¼ inch) thick. Using a medium heart cookie cutter, stamp out 12 hearts. You may need to re-roll the icing. Using small alphabet cookie cutters, lightly press the initials of the bride and groom into the hearts. Set aside and leave to dry for at least 24 hours.

Reserve 2 tablespoons of buttercream. Colour the remaining buttercream pastel purple using a few drops of pink and blue food colouring and beating with a spatula until you get the right shade.

Put the purple buttercream into a disposable piping bag with a large star nozzle and pipe a swirl of buttercream around the edge of each cupcake, lifting the nozzle up when you get to the start.

Snip the end of the piping bag off, just after the nozzle. It should leave about a 2 cm (¾ inch) opening in the piping bag. Pipe a large dollop of buttercream in the centre of each cupcake.

Put the reserved buttercream into a disposable piping bag with a small writing nozzle and pipe over the letters on each heart. When ready to serve, arrange the hearts on top of each cupcake.

Tip For an added touch, put 2 tablespoons of the purple buttercream into a piping bag with a writing nozzle. Pipe small dots around the edge of each heart.

Good luck cupcakes

Wish someone well with these simple yet totally delicious cakes. Silver horseshoes are available from most good cake shops.

Makes 12
Preparation and
decorating time:
  30 minutes + 1 hour
  setting
Cooking time:
  15–20 minutes

175 g (6 oz) **unsalted butter**,
  softened
150 g (5½ oz) **caster sugar**
3 **eggs**
175 g (6 oz) **self-raising**
  flour, sieved
½ teaspoon **baking powder**
2 tablespoons **milk**
½ teaspoon **vanilla extract**
75 g (2¾ oz) **chocolate**
  Bourbon biscuits, roughly
  chopped

To decorate
1 quantity **Runny fondant**
  icing (see page 13)
non-edible silver
  horseshoes
silver and white sugar balls

Preheat the oven to 200°C/400°F/Gas Mark 6. Line a 12-hole muffin tin with paper muffin cases.

Whisk the butter and sugar together with an electric hand whisk or beat with a wooden spoon until pale and creamy. Gradually whisk in the eggs until just combined. Using a metal spoon, fold in the flour, baking powder, milk, vanilla extract and biscuits until combined.

Divide between the paper cases and bake in the oven for 15–20 minutes until golden and risen. Leave to cool in the tin for 5 minutes, then transfer to a wire rack to go cold.

Spoon a little of the icing over each cupcake, allowing it to run and cover the top of the cakes completely. Put a horseshoe in the centre of each cake and then sprinkle with the silver and white sugar balls. Leave to set for 1 hour.

Lavender cupcakes

You can find dried lavender among the herbs and spices in the supermarkets or buy dried stems from a florist.

Makes 12
Preparation and
decorating time:
  30 minutes
Cooking time:
  20 minutes

125 ml (4 fl oz) **milk**
150 g (5½ oz) **caster sugar**
2 teaspoons **dried lavender**
150 g (5½ oz) **unsalted**
  butter
¼ teaspoon **bicarbonate of**
  soda
225 g (8 oz) **self-raising flour**
juice of ½ a **lemon**
3 **eggs**, beaten

To decorate
1 quantity **Marshmallow**
  icing (see page 12)
pink food colouring
blue food colouring
ready-made **purple sugar**
  flowers
edible crystallised violets

Preheat the oven to 180°C/350°F/Gas Mark 4. Line a 12-hole muffin tin with paper muffin cases.

Put the milk, sugar, lavender and butter in a small pan and gently heat until combined. Stir in the bicarbonate of soda and leave to cool.

Meanwhile, put the flour and lemon juice in a bowl. Add the eggs and stir with a spatula until combined. Gradually stir in the warm milk mixture.

Divide between the paper cases and bake in the oven for 20 minutes until golden and risen. Leave to cool in the tin for 5 minutes, then transfer to a wire rack to go cold.

Colour the marshmallow icing pastel purple using a few drops of pink and blue food colouring, beating with a spatula until you get the right shade.

Put a spoonful of icing on each cupcake, allowing it to run over the top. Leave it to settle for about 10 minutes then decorate with the sugar flowers and crystallised violets.

Animal cupcakes

Create your own zoo or farmyard with these great animal cakes.

Makes 12
Decorating time:
  45 minutes

300 g (10½ oz) **ready-to-roll white fondant icing**
pink food colouring
yellow food colouring
75 g (2¾ oz) **unsalted butter**, softened
150 g (5½ oz) **icing sugar**, sieved, plus extra for dusting
1 tablespoon **boiled water**, cooled, plus extra for brushing
12 **Carrot cupcakes** (see page 7)
50 g (1¾ oz) **apricot jam**, melted
ready-made **black writing icing**
brown food colouring

Equipment
7 cm (2¾ inch) round cutter
4 cm (1½ inch) round cutter
cocktail stick
shell and grass nozzles
disposable piping bags

Divide the fondant icing into three pieces. Colour one-third pink using a few drops of pink food colouring. Colour another third yellow using the yellow food colouring. Wrap all the pieces in cling film to prevent them drying out.

Whisk the butter until fluffy. Gradually add the icing sugar and about 1–2 teaspoons of the water and whisk again until light and fluffy. Set aside.

Lightly dust a clean work surface with a little icing sugar. Roll out the white fondant icing until about 3–4 mm (⅛–¼ inch) thick and, using a 7 cm (2¾ inch) round cookie cutter, stamp out four circles. You may need to re-roll the icing.

Brush the tops of four cupcakes with the apricot jam then put a white circle on the top of each cupcake, lightly pressing down. Repeat with the pink and yellow icing and remaining cupcakes. Reserve the leftover icing.

For the pig, re-roll the reserved pink icing and, using a 4 cm (1½ inch) round cookie cutter, stamp out four circles. Brush one side with a little of the water and stick just off centre on each pink cupcake. Place small triangles at the top for the ears and add small, slightly flattened balls for the snout and feet. Use a cocktail stick to make nostrils and toes. Pipe small black eyes with the writing icing and shape any leftover pink icing into a curly tail.

For the sheep, make four small balls, about the size of a Malteser, with some of the reserved white icing. Flatten slightly and stick just off centre on each white cupcake. Put the buttercream into a piping bag with a shell nozzle and pipe small shells all around the head to look like wool. Finish by making floppy ears and feet with the last of the white icing and piping eyes and a mouth using the writing icing. Use a cocktail stick to make toes.

For the lion, make four small balls, about the size of a big Malteser, with some of the reserved yellow icing. Flatten slightly and stick just off centre on each yellow cupcake. Make small balls and flatten slightly for the cheeks. Colour the remaining buttercream with the brown food colouring. Put into a piping bag with a grass nozzle and pipe a mane around the head. Pipe small black eyes and whiskers with the writing icing. Use a cocktail stick to mark the cheeks and toes.

Daisy cupcakes

This simple yet effective design can transform any cupcake. Why not give it a go with other flower shapes?

Makes 12
Decorating time:
 30 minutes

icing sugar, for dusting
150 g (5½ oz) **ready-to-roll white fondant icing**
yellow chocolate beans
1 quantity **Orange cream cheese frosting** (see variation, page 10)
12 **Raspberry swirl cupcakes** (see variation, page 7)
edible yellow glitter

Equipment
daisy flower cutter

Lightly dust a clean work surface with a little icing sugar. Roll out the fondant icing until about 3–4 mm (⅛–¼ inch) thick. Cut out 36 small daisies using a daisy-style flower cutter. You may need to re-roll the icing. Push a chocolate bean into the centre of each flower.

Using a small palette knife, spread the cream cheese frosting over the tops of the cupcakes until covered. Sprinkle the cupcakes with a little edible glitter and then top each with three daisies. Serve immediately or store in the fridge for up to 3 days.

Enchanted cupcakes

Create a fairytale land with these toadstool cakes. Why not top them with non-edible fairy cake toppers or butterflies as well.

Makes 12
Decorating time: 30 minutes + 1 hour setting

50 g (1¾ oz) **ready-to-roll white fondant icing**
15 g (½ oz) **flower paste**
icing sugar, for dusting
12 **Truly vanilla cupcakes** (see page 7)
75 g (2¾ oz) **strawberry jam**
1 quantity **Glacé icing** (see page 12)
red food colouring
70 g (2½ oz) **white chocolate buttons**

Equipment
butterfly cookie cutter

Mix together the fondant icing and the flower paste. Lightly dust a clean work surface with a little icing sugar. Roll out the fondant icing until about 3 mm (⅛ inch) thick. Then, using a small or medium butterfly cutter, stamp out a few butterflies. Make a large 'M' shape from some foil and rest the butterflies in the foil to bend the wings up slightly. Leave to dry for 1 hour.

Meanwhile, using a small, serrated knife, cut a cone shape from the top of each cake. Put a little strawberry jam into the holes and replace the cones.

Colour the glacé icing red with a few drops of red food colouring, beating with a spatula until you get the right shade. If the icing goes too runny you may need to add a little more sieved icing sugar. Put a spoonful of the icing on the top of each cupcake, allowing it to run and cover the top. Leave to set for 5–10 minutes.

Decorate the tops of the cupcakes with chocolate buttons to look like toadstools, cutting some in half and putting them around the edges. Finish with the butterflies and leave to set completely.

Tip Flower paste is a ready-made sugar paste that is ideal for making sugar flowers or other detailed figures, such as butterflies. It is available from cake shops or online.

Flower power cupcakes

You may have to sort through the chocolate beans to pick out the right colours to match your icing.

Makes 12
Decorating time:
  30 minutes

1 quantity **Lemon buttercream** (see variation, page 10)
12 **Zesty lemon cupcakes** (see page 6)
edible silver glitter
200 g (7 oz) **ready-to-roll white fondant icing**
red or **pink food colouring**
yellow food colouring
icing sugar, for dusting
pink and **orange chocolate beans** or **mini Smarties**

Equipment
large and small flower cutters
disposable piping bag

Reserving 1 tablespoon of the buttercream, spread the remainder over the tops of the cupcakes using a small palette knife. Sprinkle the tops with the silver glitter.

Divide the fondant icing into three pieces. Colour one-third with red or pink food colouring until bright pink, one-third with yellow food colouring until bright yellow and then the remaining piece with a little red and yellow food colouring until bright orange.

Roll each piece of coloured icing into a fat sausage and then press together and gently twist (like a piece of rope). Lightly dust a clean work surface with a little icing sugar and roll out the twisted icing until about 3–4 mm (1/8–1/4 inch) thick. The colours should blend together.

Using a large flower cutter, stamp out six large flowers. Using a slightly smaller flower cutter, cut out six smaller flowers. Decorate each cupcake with a flower.

Put the reserved buttercream into a piping bag and snip off the end. Pipe a dot in the centre of each flower and then stick on a chocolate bean to finish the flower.

Football cupcakes

You can find the small football players in most cake shops. Or why not try a toy shop for other small football teams?

Makes 12
Decorating time:
30 minutes

1 quantity **Lemon buttercream** (see variation, page 10)
green food colouring
12 **Zesty lemon cupcakes** (see page 6)
12 **plastic non-edible small football players**
2 **plastic non-edible small football goals**
white mimosa ball

Equipment
disposable piping bags
small star nozzle
plain writing nozzle

Reserve about 2 tablespoons of buttercream. Colour the remaining buttercream grass green using a few drops of green food colouring, beating with a spatula until you get the right shade.

Using a small palette knife, spread some of the green buttercream over the tops of the cupcakes until covered. Arrange the cupcakes on a board in a rectangle, like a football pitch.

Put the remaining green buttercream into a piping bag with a small star nozzle. Pipe small stars around the edge of the cupcake rectangle for a border, only piping on the part of each cupcake that is on the outside.

Put the reserved buttercream into a piping bag with a writing nozzle. Pipe a white line around the inside edge of the star border and dots in the corners and halfway point. Pipe two semi-circles at each end of the rectangle to make it look like a football pitch. Finally pipe a line across the middle of the rectangle, and a small circle in the centre. Decorate the cupcakes with football players and goal posts and a mimosa ball for the football.

Tip If you wish, put candles in the corner points, to look like football posts.

Spots 'v' stripes cupcakes

You can vary the colours as you wish. If you can't find the one you want, colour ready-to-roll white fondant icing using food colouring.

Makes 12
Decorating time:
 45 minutes

icing sugar, for dusting
275 g (9½ oz) **ready-to-roll white fondant icing**
50 g (1¾ oz) **ready-to-roll blue fondant icing**
12 **Zesty lemon cupcakes** (see page 6)
50 g (1¾ oz) **apricot jam,** melted
50 g (1¾ oz) **ready-to-roll green fondant icing**

Equipment
6.5 cm (2½ inch) round cutter
2.5 cm (1 inch) round cutter
1.5 cm (⅝ inch) round cutter
cocktail stick

For the striped cupcakes, lightly dust a clean work surface with a little icing sugar. Roll out 125 g (4½ oz) of white fondant icing to an 18 cm (7 inch) square about 5 mm (¼ inch) thick. Roll out the blue fondant icing to an 18 x 9 cm (7 x 3½ inch) rectangle of the same thickness.

Cut the white icing into seven and strips space them just slightly apart. Cut the blue icing into six strips and place them between the white strips, so the colours alternate. Press the strips gently together so there are no gaps. Lightly roll with a rolling pin to join the strips together.

Using a 6.5 cm (2½ inch) round cookie cutter, stamp out six circles. Brush the tops of six cupcakes with the apricot jam then put a stripy circle on the top of each, lightly pressing down.

For the spotty cupcakes, lightly dust the work surface again with a little icing sugar. Roll out the remaining white fondant then the green fondant icing until both are about 5 mm (¼ inch) thick.

Using a 2.5 cm (1 inch) and a 1.5 cm (⅝ inch) round cutter, stamp out at least 25 circles randomly from the white icing, leaving small spaces between the circles. Cut out the same number of circles from the green icing, re-rolling this icing if necessary. Reserve the circles.

Remove the white circles from their holes (if necessary) and replace with a green circle. The icing should now be white with green spots. Lightly roll with a rolling pin to join the colours.

Using a 6.5 cm (2½ inch) round cookie cutter, stamp out six circles. Brush the tops of the remaining cupcakes with the apricot jam then put a spotty circle on the top of each, lightly pressing down.

Chocolate dream cupcakes

Depending on the number of guests, why not make batches of cakes and freeze them. Then all that's left is to defrost and ice.

Makes 12
Decorating time:
  30 minutes

icing sugar, for dusting
150 g (5½ oz) **ready-to-roll chocolate fondant icing**
12 **Rich chocolate cupcakes** (see page 6)
25 g (1 oz) **apricot jam**, melted
1 quantity **Chocolate buttercream** (see variation, page 10)
edible gold glitter
ready-made **chocolate decorations** or **flowers**

Equipment
6.5 cm (2½ inch) round cutter
disposable piping bags
medium star nozzle

Lightly dust a clean work surface with a little icing sugar. Roll out the fondant icing until about 3–4 mm (⅛–¼ inch) thick. Then, using a 6.5 cm (2½ inch) round cookie cutter, stamp out six circles. You may need to re-roll the icing.

Brush the tops of six cupcakes with the apricot jam then put a circle on the top of each cupcake, lightly pressing down.

Put the buttercream into a piping bag with a medium star nozzle and pipe small stars around the edge of the iced cupcakes. Pipe stars around the edge of the remaining cupcakes. Finish with a swirl in the centre of these cupcakes.

Transfer the leftover buttercream into a disposable piping bag and snip a tiny piece off the end. Pipe four lines across the centre of four fondant iced cupcakes, crossing in the centre.

Sprinkle the cupcakes with a little edible glitter and then decorate all but those with the iced lines with a chocolate decoration or flower, using buttercream to stick them down if necessary.

18th birthday cupcakes

You could also use 21st keys for a 21st birthday. Plastic number keys can be found from most cake shops or party shops.

Makes 12
Decorating time:
  30 minutes

125 g (4½ oz) **unsalted butter**, softened
250 g (9 oz) **golden icing sugar**, sieved
2 tablespoons **boiled water**, cooled
12 **Coffee and almond cupcakes** (see page 8)
6 **non-edible plastic silver 18th number keys**
small edible silver balls
large edible silver balls

Equipment
disposable piping bag
shell nozzle

Put the butter into a bowl and whisk until fluffy. Gradually add the icing sugar and whisk until it comes together. Add the water and whisk until light and fluffy.

Put the buttercream into a piping bag with a shell nozzle and pipe shells on the cupcakes, starting on the outside edge and working your way to the centre to cover the tops.

Decorate six cupcakes with a silver key and a few small silver balls. Decorate the remaining cupcakes with large and small silver balls. Leave to set.

Tip If you prefer, you can use gold plastic keys and gold edible balls.

Ruby wedding cupcakes

Top the cakes with any ruby red sweets or sugar decorations. You could also use red sugar flowers if you liked.

Makes 12
Decorating time:
  30 minutes

icing sugar, for dusting
150 g (5½ oz) **ready-to-roll ivory fondant icing**
12 **Golden syrup cupcakes** (see variation, page 8)
25 g (1 oz) **apricot jam**, melted
100 g (3½ oz) **unsalted butter**, softened
200 g (7 oz) **golden icing sugar**, sieved
1 tablespoon **golden syrup**
edible red glitter
12 **red jelly diamonds**

Equipment
6 cm (2½ inch) crinkled round cutter
disposable piping bag
large star nozzle

Lightly dust a clean work surface with a little icing sugar. Roll out the fondant icing until about 3–4 mm (⅛–¼ inch) thick. Using a 6 cm (2½ inch) crinkled edge round cookie cutter, stamp out six circles. You may need to re-roll the icing.

Brush the tops of six cupcakes with the apricot jam then put a circle on the top of each cupcake, lightly pressing down.

Whisk the butter until fluffy. Gradually add the icing sugar and golden syrup and whisk again until light and fluffy.

Put the buttercream into a piping bag with a large star nozzle and pipe a small star in the centre of the six fondant-iced cupcakes. Pipe a large swirl on the top of the remaining cupcakes, starting from the outside edge and working your way into the centre. Sprinkle these with a little red glitter.

Put a jelly diamond on top of the buttercream on each cupcake to finish.

Sparkly cupcakes

Once you have discovered edible glitters you won't go back! Choose your favourite colours to decorate these cakes.

Makes 12
Preparation and decorating time:
 30 minutes + cooling
Cooking time:
 20–22 minutes

125 g (4½ oz) **unsalted butter**, softened
200 g (7 oz) **caster sugar**
3 **eggs**
100 ml (3½ fl oz) **double cream**
175 g (5½ oz) **self-raising flour**
75 g (2¾ oz) fresh **raspberries**
75 g (2¾ oz) fresh **blueberries**

To decorate
1 quantity **Orange buttercream** (see variation, page 10)
edible glitter
edible glitter stars

Equipment
disposable piping bag
large star nozzle

Preheat the oven to 190°C/375°F/Gas Mark 5. Line a 12-hole muffin tin with paper muffin cases.

Whisk the butter and sugar together with an electric hand whisk or beat with a wooden spoon until pale and creamy. Gradually whisk in the eggs and cream until just combined. Then add the flour, whisking again until combined and fluffy. Fold through the raspberries and blueberries.

Divide between the paper cases and bake in the oven for 20–22 minutes until golden and risen. Leave to cool in the tin for 5 minutes, then transfer to a wire rack to go cold.

Put the buttercream into a piping bag with a large star nozzle. Pipe large swirls on top of each cake, starting from the outside and working your way into the centre. Sprinkle the cakes liberally with the glitter and stars.

Ice cream cone cupcakes

These look just like the real thing but won't melt in minutes!

Makes 12
Preparation and decoration time:
  45 minutes + cooling
Cooking time:
  20–25 minutes

12 **wafer cup cornets**
125 g (4½ oz) **unsalted butter**, softened
125 g (4½ oz) **caster sugar**
1 **vanilla pod**, cut in half and seeds reserved
2 **eggs**
125 g (4½ oz) **self-raising flour**
3 tablespoons **milk**

To decorate
1 quantity **Buttercream** (see page 10)
multi-coloured sugar strands
4 **Flake bars**, each cut into 3 lengths

Equipment
disposable piping bag
large star nozzle

Preheat the oven to 190°C/375°F/Gas Mark 5. Stand the cornets in a 12-hole muffin tin – one in each muffin hole.

Whisk the butter, sugar and vanilla seeds together using an electric hand whisk or beat with a wooden spoon until pale and creamy. Gradually whisk in the eggs until just combined. Add the flour and milk and whisk again until combined and fluffy.

Divide between the cornets and bake in the oven for 20–25 minutes until golden and risen. Leave to cool in the tin for 5 minutes, then transfer to a wire rack to go cold.

Put the buttercream into a piping bag with a large star nozzle. Pipe a large swirl, just like a Mr Whippy, on to the top of each cupcake. Scatter over the sugar strands and finish each with a piece of Flake.

Tip To make it easier to fill the cornets, put the cake mixture into a disposable piping bag and snip off the end. Then pipe the mixture evenly into each cornet.

Snowflake cupcakes

You could use other Christmas shapes such as trees. Just use different cutters and red, white and green sprinkles.

Makes 12
Decorating time:
  30 minutes + 1 hour
  setting

1 quantity **Royal icing** (see
  page 13)
red food colouring
icing sugar, for dusting
75 g (2¾ oz) **ready-to-roll**
  white fondant icing
12 **Courgette and chocolate**
  cupcakes (see variation,
  page 7)
edible sugar snowflake
  sprinkles

Equipment
large snowflake cutter
disposable piping bag
large star nozzle

Colour the royal icing red with a few drops of red food colouring, beating with a spatula until you get the right shade. If the icing goes too runny you may need to add a little more sieved icing sugar.

Lightly dust a clean work surface with a little icing sugar. Roll out the fondant icing until about 3 mm (⅛ inch) thick then, using a large snowflake cutter, stamp out six snowflakes.

Put the royal icing into a piping bag with a large star nozzle and pipe a large swirl on top of each cupcake, starting from the outside and working your way into the centre. Leave to dry for about 5 minutes.

Sprinkle six cupcakes with the snowflake sprinkles. Arrange the six large snowflakes on top of the remaining cupcakes. Leave to set for 1 hour.

Drop scones

These get their name from the fact that spoonfuls of the mixture are dropped on to a hot griddle to cook them.

Makes about 24
Preparation time:
15 minutes
Cooking time:
8–10 minutes

225 g (8 oz) **plain flour**
15 g (½ oz) **caster sugar**
a pinch of **salt**
1 teaspoon **baking powder**
1 **egg**
1 teaspoon **golden syrup**
250 ml (9 fl oz) **milk**

Sift the flour, sugar, salt and baking powder into a bowl. Beat together the egg and golden syrup in a large jug.

Add the milk to the egg and syrup and stir into the dry ingredients. The batter should be like a thick cream.

Drop dessertspoons of the mixture on to a hot griddle pan or frying pan and brown both sides, turning as soon as bubbles begin to form.

Tip Often served with butter and jam, these are delicious as a savoury snack with cream cheese, smoked salmon, diced hard-boiled egg and a little mustard and cress.

Walnut and raisin bread

This recipe featured in the WI magazine *Home & Country* in March 1969 and was described as a 'winner at the children's tea'.

Serves 8
Preparation time:
 20 minutes
Baking time:
 50–60 minutes

350 g (12 oz) **wholemeal flour**
4 teaspoons **baking powder**
½ teaspoon **salt**
60 g (2 oz) **white vegetable fat**
60 g (2 oz) **caster sugar**
60 g (2 oz) **raisins**
110 g (4 oz) **walnuts**, roughly chopped
1 large **egg**
300 ml (10 fl oz) **milk**

Grease a 450 g (1 lb) loaf tin and preheat the oven to 180°C/350°F/Gas Mark 4.

Sieve the flour, baking powder and salt together into a bowl. Rub the fat into the mixture. Add the sugar, raisins and walnuts.

Beat the egg and mix it into the dry ingredients with the milk. It will be a fairly slack mixture – too soft to handle.

Spoon the mixture into the tin and bake for 50–60 minutes. Cover the top with foil towards the end of the cooking time if the top seems to be browning too quickly. Make sure it is done by inserting a skewer into the centre – if it is cooked, it will come out clean.

Cool in the tin for a few minutes and then turn out on to a wire rack.

Barley bread

In Elizabethan England, barley bread was a common option for a thrifty supper. Serve warm with lashings of butter and jam.

Serves 6
Preparation time:
  10 minutes
Baking time:
  25–30 minutes

425 g (15 oz) **barley flour**
140 g (5 oz) **plain flour**
1 teaspoon **salt**
1 teaspoon **bicarbonate of soda**
2 teaspoons **cream of tartar**
60 ml (2 fl oz) **buttermilk**

Preheat the oven to 190°C/370°F/Gas Mark 5. Place a greased baking tray in the oven.

Mix the dry ingredients together and add most of the buttermilk until the mixture forms a dough (you may not need to use all the buttermilk).

Divide the mixture into two. Roll each half out on a lightly floured surface to a 2.5 cm (1 inch) thick round. Bake on the preheated baking tray for 25–30 minutes until golden brown and cooked through.

Tips Wholegrain spelt flour can be used instead of the barley flour.

This can also be cooked on a hot griddle, turning the rounds over when the underside is cooked.

Muffins

English muffins became particularly fashionable during the 18th century. Split and serve with butter for a lovely teatime treat.

Makes 24
Preparation time:
30 minutes + about
2 hours rising
Baking time:
12–15 minutes

1.1 kg (2 lb 7 oz) **strong white bread flour**
2 teaspoons **caster sugar**
15 g (½ oz) **salt**
2½ teaspoons **fast action dried yeast**
plain flour and **semolina**, to coat

Place the flour in a large mixing bowl and stir in the sugar, salt and yeast. Make a well in the centre and pour in 600 ml (20 fl oz) of warm water. Mix to make a soft dough. Turn out on to an unfloured surface and knead for 8–10 minutes.

Place in a greased bowl and cover with oiled cling film. Set aside in a warm place to double in size for 1 hour.

Knock back, roll out to 5 mm (½ inch) thick and cut into rounds to make about 24 muffins. Place well apart on greased and floured baking trays, dust the tops with a mixture of flour and semolina and set aside in a warm place again until double in size. Preheat the oven to 220°C/425°C/Gas Mark 7.

Bake in the oven for 12–15 minutes until golden. Alternatively, cook on a greased griddle pan for about 7 minutes, cooking both sides evenly.

Notes From *More Yeast Cookery*:
'Good places to prove dough are on the rack over a stove, in the warming oven, in front of a fire or open oven door, or over a pan of warm water'.

'Bread can be set to prove three times, but the housewife usually proved bread twice, except when making "quick bread", which is only proved once.'

Potted meat

A myriad of on-the-shelf sandwich fillers have overtaken once-fashionable potted meat, but this version is all the better for being home-made.

Serves 8–10
Preparation time:
 1 hour
Cooking time: 5 hours

450 g (1 lb) **lean stewing beef**
1 teaspoon coarsely crushed **black peppercorns**
½ teaspoon **salt**
1 **allspice berry**
½ **bay leaf**
1 **mace blade** or a good grating of fresh **nutmeg**
2 teaspoons **anchovy paste** or a small tin **anchovy fillets**, drained
60 g (2 oz) **butter**, plus 25–40 g (1–1½ oz) for sealing
a little chopped fresh **parsley**

Preheat the oven to 140°C/275°F/Gas Mark 1.

Wash and dry the beef and cut into small pieces, removing any fat and sinew. Put into a greased ovenproof dish with a tight-fitting lid. Add the seasoning, all the spices and herbs and the anchovy paste or fillets and dot with the butter. Cover with the lid.

Cook for 5 hours, stirring half way through the cooking time.

Either spoon the contents into a food processor, removing the bay leaf, and blend until smooth or, for a coarse texture, chop well with a knife and fork.

Divide between ramekin dishes or spoon into one large dish. Melt the extra butter (you will need the larger amount for the ramekins), combine with the parsley and spoon over the surface.

Tip Sealing with butter allows you to keep the potted meat for up to a week in the fridge.

Variation For added flavour, try adding a little garlic, chopped fresh rosemary, some of your favourite fresh herbs, or even a splash of sherry.

Mini sausage and egg pies

These delicious little pies are a variation on pork pies and should be made the day before they are eaten. The savoury jelly can be omitted if you wish.

Makes 4
Preparation time:
  30–40 minutes
Cooking time:
  30–35 minutes

2 **eggs**
250 g (9 oz) **puff pastry**,
  defrosted if frozen
400 g (14 oz) **pork sausage**
  meat or 6 **pork sausages**,
  skinned
½ teaspoon **mixed herbs**
½ teaspoon **Home-made**
  mustard (page 91)
salt and freshly ground
  black pepper
1 **egg**, beaten, to seal
  and glaze

Savoury jelly
140 ml (5 fl oz) **meat stock**
½ heaped tablespoon
  gelatine

To make the savoury jelly, put the meat stock and gelatine into a saucepan. Stir over a gentle heat until every grain of gelatine has disappeared. Season well. Use when the jelly is cool. You will only need some of the jelly. Preheat the oven to 200°C/400°F/Gas Mark 6.

Add the eggs to a small pan of water, bring to the boil and simmer for 6 minutes. Rinse with cold water and peel.

Cut the pastry into four pieces. From each piece keep back one-third for the lid. Roll out the pastry and use to line four 10 cm (4 inch) wide, 3 cm (1¼ inch) deep Yorkshire pudding tins. Roll out the lids.

Mix the sausage meat, mixed herbs and mustard together and season.

Cut the hard-boiled eggs in half and place a half in the bottom of each case, cut side down. Top with the sausage meat.

Brush the edges of the pies with the beaten egg, position the lids and press well together. Cut into the edges with a sharp knife to decorate. Make a small hole in the centre of each pie.

Using the pastry trimmings, make two or three leaves for each pie and a little pastry rose to go round each hole in the middle. Brush with beaten egg to glaze.

Cook for 30–35 minutes until the pastry is golden brown. Cool in the tins. When cool, lift the roses off the pies and fill each with cooling jelly, if using. Chill.

Tip A pinch of salt in the beaten egg makes a very glossy glaze.

Scotch eggs

Rumour has it that these were invented by Fortnum & Mason in 1738. They're traditionally served cold and are having something of a revival.

Makes 6
Preparation time:
  20 minutes
Cooking time:
  18–24 minutes

6 **eggs**
400 g (14 oz) **pork sausage meat**
2 tablespoons **plain flour**
salt and freshly ground **black pepper**
1 **egg**, beaten
8 tablespoons **breadcrumbs**
vegetable oil, for deep frying
watercress or **parsley**, to garnish

Add the eggs to a small pan of water, bring to the boil and simmer for 6 minutes. Rinse with cold water and peel while still hot. Cool in cold water.

Divide the sausage meat into six equal pieces and pat out into rounds.

Put some flour on a plate, season, dip each egg in the flour and cover with the sausage meat.

Flour again, dip in the beaten egg and roll in the breadcrumbs.

Heat the oil in a deep heavy-bottomed pan until it reaches 180°C/350°F on a sugar thermometer or until a breadcrumb sizzles and turns brown when dropped into the oil. Cook two eggs at a time for 6–8 minutes until golden brown. Wait for the oil to heat up again before cooking the next batch.

Carefully drain with a slotted spoon on to kitchen towel. Cut into halves and serve garnished with watercress or parsley.

Tips To cook in the oven, place on a baking tray and bake at 190°C/375°F/Gas Mark 5 for 25 minutes until golden brown.

To make these even more tasty, use skinned gourmet sausages instead of the sausage meat. Try garlicky Toulouse sausages, pork and apple, or pork, pancetta and Parmesan.

Quiche Lorraine

Quiche Lorraine became popular in Britain after World War II and features in most WI recipe books. This recipe is delicious served hot or cold.

Serves 6–8
Preparation time:
  30 minutes +
  45–50 minutes
  chilling
Cooking time:
  65 minutes

6 rashers **streaky bacon,**
  rind removed
1 small **onion,** finely
  chopped
110 g (4 oz) mature **Cheddar**
  cheese, grated
2 **eggs**
150 ml (5 fl oz) **full-fat milk**
  or **single cream**
25 g (1 oz) **butter,** melted
salt and freshly ground
  black pepper
a little **cayenne pepper**

Pastry
80 g (3 oz) **butter**
175 g (6 oz) **plain flour**

To make the pastry, rub the butter into the flour until it resembles breadcrumbs. Add enough cold water to make the crumb mixture come together to form a firm dough, wrap in cling film and chill in the fridge for 30 minutes.

Roll out the pastry on a lightly floured surface and line a well-greased 22 cm (8½ inch) flan dish. Chill again for 15–20 minutes. Preheat the oven to 190°C/375°F/Gas Mark 5.

Remove the pastry from the fridge, line the base with baking parchment and then fill it with baking beans. Place on a baking tray and bake blind for 20 minutes. Remove the beans and parchment and return to the oven for another 5 minutes to dry and crisp the base. Remove from the oven and increase the temperature to 200°C/400°F/Gas Mark 6.

Meanwhile, fry the bacon lightly with the onion. Cut the rashers in half and cover the pastry with the bacon, onion and cheese.

Beat the eggs, cream and melted butter together and season with salt, pepper and a little cayenne pepper.

Pour over the bacon mixture and bake for 40 minutes until set and golden brown.

Harvest sausage rolls

These are a far cry from processed sausage rolls bought in a supermarket. The pastry can be lightened by using half plain and half wholemeal flour.

**Makes 10–14,
   depending on size**
**Preparation time:
   20 minutes +
   30 minutes chilling
Cooking time:
   20–30 minutes**

60 g (2 oz) **margarine**
60 g (2 oz) **white vegetable
   fat**
225 g (8 oz) **plain
   wholemeal flour**
a pinch of **salt**
1 **egg**, beaten
225 g (8 oz) **pork sausage
   meat**
½ teaspoon **dried sage**
25 g (1 oz) **bran**
Home-made mustard, to
   serve (see recipe)

Preheat the oven to 200°C/400°F/Gas Mark 6.

Make the pastry by rubbing both fats into the flour and salt in a large bowl. Add about 60 ml (2 fl oz) of cold water, or enough to bring the mixture together to form a dough. Wrap in cling film and chill for 30 minutes.

Roll out half the pastry to a 20 × 10 cm (11 × 4 inch) strip. Do the same with the other half. Leave the strips to relax while you prepare the filling.

Mix half the egg into the sausage meat with the sage. Wash and dry your hands and dust in wholemeal flour (or use latex gloves). Mould the sausage meat into two rolls the length of the pastry strips. Put one on each of the strips.

Brush a little beaten egg along one edge of each strip and fold over. Press the edges firmly together. Brush each roll with the remaining beaten egg and sprinkle with the bran. Cut diagonally to make individual sausage rolls. Put on a baking tray and bake for 20–30 minutes. Cool on a wire rack and eat hot or cold with mustard.

Home-made mustard
Home-made mustard makes these special sausage rolls even more delicious.

50 g (1¾ oz) each **black** and **white
   mustard seeds**
150 ml (5 fl oz) **herb vinegar**
3 tablespoons runny **honey**
1 teaspoon **salt**
½ teaspoon **mace**

Put all the ingredients into a bowl and leave overnight to soften the seeds.

Mix in a blender until thick and creamy. If too thick, add a little more vinegar. Leave a proportion of the seeds whole – do not blend until there are no seeds to be seen.

Store in small jars with plastic lids. Keep airtight or the mustard will dry out.

Vary the flavour with different spices, vinegars and more or less honey.

Anchovy eggs

An interesting Breconshire variation on traditional egg mayonnaise. The anchovy gives a piquant flavour to the eggs.

Serves 4
Preparation time:
  25 minutes

4 hard-boiled **eggs**, peeled
a little **salt**
a little **cayenne pepper**
2 teaspoons **anchovy essence**
2 tablespoons **mayonnaise**
8 small slices **brown bread**
butter
2 **tomatoes**, each cut into 4 slices, discarding the ends
a little fresh **parsley**, to garnish

Halve the eggs and remove the yolks. Place the yolks in a bowl with a little salt and cayenne pepper, the anchovy essence and mayonnaise and mix it all together to create a moist paste.

Spoon the paste into a piping bag and pipe it back into the egg whites. Alternatively, spoon the mixture straight into the cavities.

Butter the bread and cut into small rounds. Place a thin round of tomato on each round and half an egg on top. Garnish with a little fresh parsley.

Pinwheel sandwiches

An attractive and practical way to serve sandwiches for a party. Each filling is sufficient for one large loaf.

Makes 80–120 pinwheels
Preparation time: 45 minutes + chilling

1 large **white** or **brown tin loaf**, uncut and chilled for ease of cutting
about 175 g (6 oz) **butter**, softened, or **low-fat spread**

Crab and gherkin filling
2–3 large jars **crab paste**
jar midget **gherkins**

Egg and cress filling
6 **eggs**
3–4 tablespoons **mayonnaise**
3 cartons **mustard and cress**, chopped
salt and freshly ground **black pepper**

Cut off the crust all round the loaf. Cut off a 1-cm (½-inch) thick slice from the long side, keeping it even. Repeat to get 10 slices. A good baker can do this for you. Butter each slice of bread.

For the crab and gherkin pinwheels, spread each slice with crab paste and then arrange a line of drained midget gherkins along one short edge. Roll up tightly, beginning at the edge with the gherkins, wrap at once in cling film and refrigerate until required. Slice each roll into 8–12 pinwheels.

For the egg and cress pinwheels, add the eggs to a small pan of water, bring to the boil and simmer for 6 minutes. Rinse with cold water and peel. Cool the hard-boiled eggs in cold water and then dry on kitchen towel. Mash finely, adding the mayonnaise, mustard and cress and seasoning. Spread each slice with this mixture, roll up, wrap in cling film and refrigerate until required. Slice each roll into 8–12 pinwheels.

Tip Make these the day before to make sure they hold together, then simply cut into slices when required.

Whitstable sandwiches

The coastal town of Whitstable in Kent is famed for its seafood. Spread this quick and tasty filling between slices of buttered bread or on pieces of toast.

Serves 4
Preparation time:
  15 minutes + 2 hours
  marinating

250 g (9 oz) cooked, peeled
  shrimp or **prawns**
2 **spring onions,** sliced
2 tablespoons **French**
  dressing
3 **eggs**
2 tablespoons finely
  chopped **lettuce**
2 tablespoons finely
  chopped **watercress**
Old-fashioned salad cream
  (see recipe)
8 slices **wholemeal bread**
butter, softened

Cover the shrimps or prawns and spring onions with the French dressing and leave to marinate for 2 hours.

Meanwhile, add the eggs to a small pan of water, bring to the boil and simmer for 6 minutes. Rinse with cold water and peel. Cool in cold water, dry on kitchen towel and halve.

Separate the egg yolks from the whites. Pass the yolks through a sieve to mash them and chop the whites finely. Mix into the shrimp or prawn mixture with the lettuce and watercress and a little salad cream.

Butter the bread and divide the mixture between four of the slices. Top with the remaining slices and cut into triangles.

Old-fashioned salad cream
This recipe from food writer Margaret Ryan featured in the WI magazine *Home & Country* in July 1969.

25 g (1 oz) **plain flour**
2 tablespoons **caster sugar**
1 teaspoon **salt**
½ teaspoon freshly ground **black pepper**
1 **egg**
1 tablespoon **English mustard powder**
1 tablespoon **sunflower** or **extra virgin**
  olive oil
600 ml (20 fl oz) **milk**
150 ml (5 fl oz) **white wine vinegar**

Sift the flour, sugar, salt and pepper into a bowl. Beat the egg in another bowl, add the mustard and the oil and beat again. Add the milk, stirring well all the time. Add the milk mixture gradually to the flour, making a thin paste and then stirring in the rest. If you have a blender, give it a whizz.

Pour into a small saucepan and place over a moderate heat. Cook, stirring all the time, until it boils. Continue to cook for 3–4 minutes, stirring constantly. When the mixture is very thick, smooth and creamy, take it off the heat and let it cool for a few moments before adding the vinegar and giving it a final whisk.

Cornish potato cake

This 'winter teatime savoury' is not quite as famous as the Cornish pasty, but it's a great way to use up your potatoes.

Serves 6–8
Preparation time:
30 minutes
Cooking time:
20–30 minutes

450 g (1 lb) peeled **potatoes** (weighed after peeling)
salt
110 g (4 oz) **plain flour**
60 g (2 oz) **butter**
white pepper

Boil the potatoes in lightly salted water until they are cooked. Strain and tip into a bowl. Preheat the oven to 220°C/425°F/Gas Mark 7.

Add the flour and butter to the hot potatoes and mash thoroughly together. Season with salt and white pepper.

Spoon on to a greased baking tray and press out with your hands to about 5 mm (¼ inch) thick. Score the top criss-cross wise with a fork and bake in the oven for 20–30 minutes until nicely browned.

Cut into pieces and serve at once.

Tip Alternatively, you could cut the potato cakes into circles using a saucer and bake individually on a tray.

Victoria sandwich

Sweet, fluffy, and unmistakably British – the Victoria sandwich still reigns supreme at village fêtes and on afternoon tea menus across the nation.

Serves 6
Preparation time:
 20 minutes
Baking time:
 25–30 minutes

110 g (4 oz) soft **margarine**
110 g (4 oz) **caster sugar**,
 plus extra for decorating
2 **eggs**
110 g (4 oz) **self-raising flour**
raspberry jam, for filling

Preheat the oven to 180°C/350°F/Gas Mark 4. Grease two 15 cm (6 inch) sandwich tins and line with non-stick baking parchment or greased greaseproof paper.

Cream the margarine and sugar together until light and creamy in texture.

Add the eggs a little at a time and beat well. Sift the flour and gently fold into the mixture.

Divide the mixture between the two prepared tins and bake in the oven for 25–30 minutes until well risen and the tops spring back when lightly pressed with a fingertip.

When cold, fill with jam and sprinkle the top with caster sugar.

Variations This recipe is taken from the *Cumbria–Cumberland WI Cookery Book* and can be adapted to make 20 small sweet buns.

Queen cakes – add 40 g (1½ oz) of currants.

Coffee – add 1 teaspoon of coffee essence or coffee water.

Walnut – add 60 g (2 oz) of chopped walnuts.

Orange – add the grated zest of ½ an orange.

Chocolate fudge cake

A rich chocolatey cake based on a recipe from the *Northumberland WI Cookery Book*, 1969. The chocolate fudge icing is a delicious addition.

Makes 20 squares
Preparation time:
  20 minutes + cooling
Baking time:
  25–30 minutes

40 g (1½ oz) **cocoa powder**
5 tablespoons boiling **water**
175 g (6 oz) soft **margarine**
  or **butter**
175 g (6 oz) **caster sugar**
3 **eggs**
1 teaspoon **vanilla essence**
175 g (6 oz) **self-raising flour**
1½ teaspoons **baking
  powder**
crystallised rose petals,
  crushed, to decorate

Chocolate fudge icing
100 g (3½ oz) **plain
  chocolate** (70% cocoa
  solids), broken into pieces
60 g (2 oz) **butter**, diced
2 tablespoons **double cream**

Preheat the oven to 180°C/350°F/Gas Mark 4. Line an 18 x 28 cm (7 x 11 inch) roasting tin or cake tin with a large piece of non-stick baking parchment, snipping diagonally into the corners of the paper and pressing into the tin so that the base and sides are lined.

Place the cocoa powder in a small bowl, gradually mix in the boiling water until you get a smooth paste and set aside to cool.

Cream the margarine or butter and sugar together until light and fluffy. Gradually beat in the eggs and vanilla essence with a spoonful of the flour.

Mix the remaining flour with the baking powder and then stir into the mixture with the cooled cocoa paste until smooth.

Spoon into the prepared tin, spread into an even layer and bake for 25–30 minutes until well risen and the top springs back when lightly pressed with a fingertip.

Leave to cool for 10 minutes and then lift the cake from the tin using the paper. Peel down the paper on the sides and leave to cool on a wire rack

To make the icing, melt the chocolate in a bowl over a pan of simmering water. Add the butter and stir to melt. Add the cream and stir until smooth and glossy.

Spread the icing over the cake, sprinkle with crushed crystallised rose petals and leave to set. Cut into 20 pieces, lift off the base paper and transfer to a serving plate. Serve in cupcake cases, if liked.

Madeira cake

This buttery lemon sponge is delicious taken with tea or with a mid-morning glass of Madeira wine.

Serves 8
Preparation time:
  20 minutes + cooling
Baking time:
  35–40 minutes

110 g (4 oz) **butter**, softened
110 g (4 oz) **caster sugar**
a pinch of **salt**
3 **eggs**, lightly beaten
140 g (5 oz) **self-raising flour**
finely grated zest of 1 **lemon**

Preheat the oven to 180°C/350°F/Gas Mark 4. Grease a 15 cm (6 inch) round cake tin and line with non-stick baking parchment or greased greaseproof paper.

Beat the butter and sugar together with the salt until very light and creamy.

Add the eggs one at a time, beating each one in thoroughly. Lastly, fold in the flour and lemon zest.

Pour the cake mixture into the prepared tin and bake for 35–40 minutes until well risen and the top springs back when lightly pressed with a fingertip. Turn out on a wire rack to cool.

Tip This mixture can be used as a base for a fruit cake – just add 110 g (4 oz) of currants, 60 g (2 oz) of sultanas and a little mixed peel.

Saffron cake

Yellow saffron cake is as much a delicacy in Cornwall as the Cornish pasty. It is popularly believed that the Phoenicians first brought it to the country.

Serves 8
Preparation time:
20 minutes + proving + cooling
Baking time:
50 minutes

200 ml (7 fl oz) warm **milk** or half and half warm **milk** and **water**
25 g (1 oz) **fast action dried yeast**
175 g (6 oz) **caster sugar**
900 g (2 lb) **plain flour**
350 g (12 oz) **butter**
1 teaspoon **salt**
60 g (2 oz) **mixed peel**
450 g (1 lb) **currants**
1 teaspoon **saffron**

Place the warm milk or milk and water in a bowl and add the yeast, 1 teaspoon of the sugar and a couple of heaped spoonfuls of the flour. Stir, cover and set aside,

In a large bowl, rub the butter into the remaining flour until the mixture resembles breadcrumbs and then mix in the salt, peel, currants and remaining sugar.

Roll the saffron between two pieces of greaseproof paper to crumble it and then steep it in a little hot water. Add to the cake mixture with the yeast and liquid mixture to form a dough.

Knead well on an unfloured work surface for 8–10 minutes. Some of the currants will escape – simply put them back in the dough at the end of kneading. Cover with oiled cling film or a clean, damp tea towel and set aside until doubled in size (the time this takes will depend on the warmth of the room).

Knead again. Grease a 900 g (2 lb) loaf tin and put the dough in the tin to prove. Cover with oiled cling film or a clean, damp tea towel and set aside until doubled in size again. Preheat the oven to 190°C/375°F/Gas Mark 5.

Bake for 25 minutes and then reduce the temperature to 180°C/350°F/Gas Mark 4 and bake for a further 25 minutes. Cool in the tin for a few minutes before turning out on to a wire rack.

Fruity marmalade cake

The addition of marmalade to this fruit cake gives it a subtle spicy flavour. Don't worry if your fruit sinks a little – it will still taste great.

Serves 8
Preparation time:
  30 minutes + cooling
  Baking time: 1 hour
  50 minutes–2 hours

225 g (8 oz) **self-raising flour**
¼ level teaspoon **mixed spice**
¼ level teaspoon grated **nutmeg**
¼ level teaspoon **cinnamon**
a pinch of **salt**
110 g (4 oz) **caster sugar**
60 g (2 oz) **glacé cherries**, chopped
225 g (8 oz) dried **mixed fruit**
1 heaped tablespoon thick **orange marmalade**
3 **eggs**
6 tablespoons **milk**
a few drops of **vanilla extract**
110 g (4 oz) **butter**, melted
15 g (½ oz) **walnuts**, chopped

Preheat the oven to 150°C/300°F/Gas Mark 2.

Grease an 18 cm (7 inch) round cake tin, line with non-stick baking parchment or greased greaseproof paper and tie a piece of brown paper around the outside of the tin so that it stands about 5 cm (2 inches) above the tin.

Sift the flour, spices, salt and sugar into a bowl, add the cherries, dried fruit and marmalade and stir well.

Break the eggs one at a time into a jug and stir into the mixture. Add the milk, vanilla extract and melted butter.

Mix thoroughly and then beat with a wooden spoon for 3 minutes. Turn the mixture into the prepared tin.

Sprinkle the top of the mixture with the chopped walnuts and bake in the centre of the oven for 1 hour 50 minutes–2 hours. Check that the cake is cooked by inserting a skewer into the centre of the cake. If it comes out clean, the cake is ready.

Leave to cool in the tin for 30 minutes and then turn out on to a wire rack.

Carrot cake

This cake was revived in World War II as carrots were a cheap and healthy alternative to sugar and sweetened products.

Serves 8–12
Preparation time:
  30 minutes + cooling
Baking time: 40–45
  minutes

175 g (6 oz) soft **margarine**
110 g (4 oz) **light muscovado**
  sugar
2 eggs
250 g (9 oz) **self-raising flour**
½ teaspoon **ground**
  cinnamon
25 g (1 oz) **mixed peel** or
  marmalade
finely grated zest of
  1 orange
60 g (2 oz) **raisins**, washed
225 g (8 oz) finely grated
  carrots
4–5 tablespoons **milk** or
  orange juice

Cream cheese frosting
170 g (6 oz) **cream cheese**
60 g (2 oz) soft **margarine** or
  butter
110 g (4 oz) **icing sugar**
a few drops **vanilla extract**

Preheat the oven to 180°C/350°F/Gas Mark 4. Lightly grease an 18 cm (7 inch) square or a 20 cm (8 inch) round cake tin.

Cream the margarine with the sugar until light and creamy. Whisk the eggs and beat into the mixture.

Sieve the flour with the cinnamon and fold into the creamed mixture together with the peel or marmalade, orange zest and raisins.

Mix in the grated carrots. Add sufficient milk or orange juice to give a dropping consistency. Pour the mixture into the prepared tin and smooth over the top.

Bake for 40–45 minutes until golden brown, firm to the touch and a skewer comes out clean when inserted into the centre of the cake. Cool in the tin for 15 minutes and then turn out on to a wire rack.

For the frosting, cream together the cream cheese and margarine or butter and then beat in the icing sugar and vanilla extract. Use to cover the top of the cake and then cut into 8–12 servings.

Tip Decorate with bought sugar carrot decorations or make your own with ready-to-roll orange and green fondant icing.

Génoise sponge cake

A Génoise cake is a whisked sponge enriched with melted butter. It is the perfect base for gâteaux and petits fours.

Serves 6–8
Preparation time:
  30 minutes + cooling
Baking time:
  20–30 minutes

4 eggs
125 g (4½ oz) **caster sugar**
100 g (3½ oz) **fine plain flour**
100 g (3½ oz) **butter**

Preheat the oven to 180°C/350°F/Gas Mark 4. Lightly oil a 20 cm (8 inch) cake tin and line it carefully with non-stick baking parchment or greased greaseproof paper.

Break the eggs into a large bowl, add the sugar and whisk over a pan of simmering water until the mixture has almost doubled in bulk and the whisk leaves a heavy trail. Take off the heat and continue to whisk for a minute or two.

Sift the flour twice to incorporate as much air as possible. Melt the butter in a small pan and cool until just runny. Fold the flour into the mixture with the melted butter. Mix swiftly but gently.

Turn into the prepared tin and cook for 20–30 minutes until the cake is just shrinking from the sides of the tin. Turn out on to a cloth, invert on to a wire rack and leave to cool.

Tip This is delicious filled with cream and jam and/or fruit.

Cherry cake

If you wash the cherries in warm water and dry thoroughly, this takes away the stickiness that is apt to make them sink to the bottom of the cake.

Serves 8
Preparation time:
  25 minutes + cooling
Baking time: 1 hour
  30 minutes

175 g (6 oz) **butter**, softened
175 g (6 oz) **caster sugar**,
  plus 1 level tablespoon
  for decoration
3 **eggs**, beaten
250 g (9 oz) **plain flour**
2½ level teaspoons **baking
  powder**
1 tablespoon **milk**
350 g (12 oz) **glacé cherries**,
  quartered but leaving 3
  whole

Preheat the oven to 190°C/375°F/Gas Mark 5. Grease a 15 cm (6 inch) square cake tin and line with non-stick baking parchment or greased greaseproof paper.

Beat the butter to a soft cream and then beat in the caster sugar. Add the eggs to the mixture, a little at a time.

Sieve the flour and baking powder together and stir lightly into the mixture with the milk. Add the quartered cherries and stir them evenly through the mixture.

Turn into the prepared tin. Smooth the top and make a slight hollow in the centre. Sprinkle the tablespoon of sugar on top. Cut the three remaining cherries in half and dot them over the top.

Bake in the centre of the oven for 20 minutes, then reduce the temperature to 180°C/350°F/ Gas Mark 4 and bake for a further 40 minutes. Lastly, reduce the temperature again to 150°C/300°F/Gas Mark 2 and bake for 30 minutes.

Leave to cool in the tin for 10 minutes and then turn out on to a wire rack.

Coffee cake

Bringing an air of sophistication to afternoon tea, no teatime gathering is complete without a slice of coffee cake.

Serves 8
Preparation time:
30 minutes + cooling
Baking time:
20–25 minutes

175 g (6 oz) **butter**, softened
175 g (6 oz) **light brown soft sugar**
1 tablespoon strong **coffee** (see Tip) or a few drops of **coffee essence**
3 **eggs**, lightly beaten
175 g (6 oz) **self-raising flour**
1 teaspoon **baking powder**

Butter cream
110 g (4 oz) **butter**, softened
225 g (8 oz) **icing sugar**
2 tablespoons strong **coffee** (see Tip) or 1 teaspoon **coffee essence**
80 g (3 oz) **walnuts**, chopped

To decorate
icing sugar
8 **walnut halves**

Preheat the oven to 180°C/350°F/Gas Mark 4. Grease two 20 cm (8 inch) sandwich tins and base line with non-stick baking parchment or greased greaseproof paper.

Cream the butter and sugar together, add the coffee and beat in the eggs little by little, keeping the mixture stiff. Sift the flour and baking powder together and fold in.

Divide the mixture between the prepared tins and bake for 20–25 minutes until risen and the tops spring back when lightly pressed with a fingertip.

Allow to cool in the tins for a few minutes then turn out, peel away the paper and cool on a wire rack.

Make the butter cream by blending the butter, icing sugar and coffee together until smooth.

Take one cake and arrange wooden skewers over the top to mark out eight portions. Sieve icing sugar over the top and then remove the skewers. Pipe on eight butter cream rosettes and top each with a walnut piece.

Add the chopped walnuts to the remaining butter cream and spread over the second cake. Put the first cake on top of this.

Tip Strong coffee for the cake and butter cream can be made from 2 teaspoons of instant coffee dissolved in 3 tablespoons of boiling water.

Party rings

Light rings of choux pastry filled with fresh fruit and cream complete any tea table. You could also fill these with nectarines or strawberries.

Makes 6
Preparation time:
  35 minutes
Baking time:
  20–25 minutes

2 ripe **peaches**
boiling water
275 ml (10 fl oz) **whipping** or **double cream**, whipped
150 g (5½ oz) **raspberries**
100 g (3½ oz) **icing sugar**

Choux pastry
60 g (2 oz) **butter**, diced
70 g (2½ oz) **strong white flour**
1 teaspoon **caster sugar**
2 **eggs**, beaten

Preheat the oven to 200°C/400°F/Gas Mark 6. Put the oven shelf in the top half of the oven if your oven isn't fan assisted. Grease a baking tray.

To make the choux pastry, put 150 ml (5 fl oz) of cold water and the butter in a saucepan. Place over a medium heat until the butter has melted and it all comes to the boil. Meanwhile, sieve the flour on to a sheet of baking parchment that has been folded in half.

Remove the butter water from the heat and 'shoot' the flour into the mixture with the sugar. Beat vigorously with a wooden spoon (or use an electric hand whisk) until you have a smooth ball of paste.

Add the eggs gradually, beating well between each addition until the paste is smooth and glossy. Spoon the mixture into a piping bag with a 1 cm (½ inch) plain nozzle. Sprinkle water on to the baking tray and tap to get rid of any excess.

Pipe the pastry into six 7.5 cm (3 inch) circles. Bake for 15–20 minutes until well risen and golden brown.

Make a small slit in each ring to let the steam escape and return to the oven for a couple of minutes to dry out the centres. Set aside on a wire rack to cool.

Dip the peaches in boiling water. Skin them and cut them into small pieces. Split the rings in half and fill the bottom half of the pastry ring with the whipped cream. Top with the peaches and raspberries and replace the lid.

Mix the icing sugar with 3–4 teaspoons of water to make a glacé icing. Drizzle the icing over the rings to decorate.

Tip The pastry rings can be made in the morning or the day before. Put them into an absolutely airtight tin when cold. They can then be filled just before the party.

Chocolate walnut cake

Chocolate is an unusual addition in this lightly spiced fruit cake but works extremely well – an absolute delight.

Serves 8–12
Preparation time:
 25 minutes + cooling
Baking time: 1½ hours

350 g (12 oz) **self-raising flour**
½ teaspoon **ground cinnamon**
½ teaspoon **mixed spice**
175 g (6 oz) soft **margarine**
60 g (2 oz) **walnuts**, roughly chopped
60 g (2 oz) **plain chocolate** (70% cocoa solids), roughly chopped
175 g (6 oz) **raisins**
175 g (6 oz) **demerara sugar**, plus 1 tablespoon for the topping
2 **eggs**, beaten
about 150 ml (5 fl oz) **milk**

Preheat the oven to 180°C/350°F/Gas Mark 4. Lightly grease a 20 cm (8 inch) round or an 18 cm (7 inch) square cake tin and line with non-stick baking parchment or greased greaseproof paper.

Sieve the flour and spices into a mixing bowl and rub in the margarine. Stir the walnuts, chocolate and raisins into the mixture, together with the sugar.

Stir the eggs into the dry ingredients, together with three-quarters of the milk. Mix thoroughly, adding enough of the remaining milk to give a soft dropping consistency.

Place in the prepared tin, smooth over the top and sprinkle with the sugar for the topping.

Bake for 1 hour and then reduce the oven temperature to 150°C/300°F/Gas Mark 2. Bake for a further 30 minutes until the cake is firm to the touch and a skewer inserted in the centre comes out clean.

Cool the cake in the tin for 10–15 minutes and then turn out on to a wire rack.

Meringue-topped cake

An unusual cake to delight your guests, the cherries and almonds add an extra delicious touch.

Serves 8
Preparation time:
  20 minutes
Baking time:
  25–30 minutes

175 g (6 oz) **self-raising flour**
¼ teaspoon **baking powder**
80 g (3 oz) soft **margarine** or **butter**
60 g (2 oz) **light brown soft sugar**
2 **eggs,** separated
110 g (4 oz) **icing sugar,** sieved
60 g (2 oz) **glacé cherries,** halved
25 g (1 oz) **flaked almonds**

Preheat the oven to 190°C/375°F/Gas Mark 5. Lightly grease a 25 x 18 cm (10 x 7 inch) or 20 cm (8 inch) round cake tin and line with non-stick baking parchment or greased greaseproof paper.

Sieve the flour and baking powder into a bowl, rub in the margarine or butter and mix in the sugar and egg yolks. Pour the mixture into the prepared tin.

Whisk the egg whites in a clean bowl until stiff peaks form. Fold in the icing sugar.

Spread the meringue mixture on top of the cake mixture and decorate with the cherries and flaked almonds.

Bake fairly near the top of the oven for 25–30 minutes, moving down to a middle shelf for the last 5 minutes. You may need to cover the top loosely with foil if the meringue browns too quickly.

Note This recipe is taken from the *Derbyshire WI Recipe Book*, a collection of recipes welcomed as a further contribution towards the development of the 'basis of all good housekeeping', reads the foreword. 'The countrywoman's reputation as a "good cook" is proverbial and the recipes contained in this book reflect the art and experience which has rightly and justly earned this reputation.'

Golden layer cake

Celebrate a special occasion with this regal cake from an old Yorkshire recipe. Don't be put off by all the stages – this is outstandingly good!

Serves 6–8
Preparation and baking time: 1 hour 25–30 minutes

110 g (4 oz) **butter** or **margarine**, softened
110 g (4 oz) **light brown soft sugar**
225 g (8 oz) **plain flour**
1 level teaspoon **baking powder**
½ teaspoon **ground cinnamon**
½ teaspoon **ground nutmeg**
2 whole **eggs** and 1 **egg yolk**
150 ml (5 fl oz) **golden syrup**
70 ml (3 fl oz) **milk**

To decorate
1 tablespoon **golden syrup**
225 g (8 oz) **icing sugar**
3 dessertspoons **apricot jam**
25 g (1 oz) **walnuts**, chopped
175 g (6 oz) **light brown soft sugar**
1 **egg** white
1 teaspoon **vanilla extract**
walnut halves

Preheat the oven to 180°C/350°F/ Gas Mark 4. Grease two 20 cm (8 inch) deep loose-bottomed sandwich tins.

Beat the butter or margarine and sugar together until soft and creamy.

Sift the flour with the baking powder and spices. Whisk the whole eggs and egg yolk together. Heat the golden syrup slightly by warming it in the microwave for 20 seconds and add to the whisked eggs. Whisk together.

Gradually add the flour and egg mixtures into the creamed fat and sugar, alternating them, mixing well and adding the milk to moisten.

Divide the mixture between the two prepared tins, spread evenly and bake for 25–30 minutes, turning the cakes during cooking to make sure they rise evenly. Leave to rest for a few moments before turning out of the tins and setting aside to cool.

For the first filling, warm the golden syrup and mix with 1 dessertspoon of hot water. Add this to the icing sugar with enough extra hot water to make a thick coating consistency.

For the second filling, mix the jam and chopped walnuts together. If the jam is very stiff, it may need to be warmed slightly.

Halve each cake and cover one half of each with the syrup and sugar filling, pouring it into the centre and spreading it to the edge. Sandwich together again. Now sandwich the two whole cakes together with a thick layer of the jam and walnut filling.

To make the icing, put the brown sugar in a large mixing bowl with 35 ml (1 fl oz) of cold water and add the egg white and vanilla extract. Whisk together over hot water, preferably using an electric hand whisk, until the mixture becomes stiff. Spread a thin layer over the top and sides of the cake to stick the crumbs in place and then spoon over generously and spread into swirls with a round bladed knife. Leave until set and decorate with the walnut halves.

Tip Test a little of the icing on a plate to see if it will set before spreading it on the cake. If it is not ready, whisk for a little longer.

Festival tartlets

Dark chocolate cases filled with moist raspberry sponge – utterly decadent.
You could cheat by buying the chocolate cases.

Makes 8
Preparation time:
  **30 minutes + 2 hours
  chilling**

110 g (4 oz) **plain chocolate**
  (70% cocoa solids),
  broken into pieces
110 g (4 oz) **sponge cake**,
  crumbled
2 tablespoons **raspberry
  jam**
1 tablespoon **Kirsch** or
  brandy
125 ml (4 fl oz) **whipping
  cream**, whipped
8 **raspberries** or **cherries**
angelica, cut into leaf
  shapes (optional)

Place the chocolate in a bowl over a pan of simmering water and stir until melted. Brush eight cupcake paper cases (use two together if flimsy) with the melted chocolate, making sure it is in an even layer. Leave to set for 10 minutes and then brush the insides of the cases again with chocolate, re-melting if necessary and again making sure it is in an even layer. Chill for a couple of hours.

Mix the crumbled sponge cake with the jam and Kirsch to give a soft consistency.

Carefully peel the paper cases away from the chocolate and divide the cake mixture between the chocolate cases.

Decorate with the whipped cream, raspberries or cherries and angelica leaves, if using.

Tip Put the chocolate-coated paper cases in a bun tin to set. This will help them set to a nice round shape.

Birthday cake

This is a special occasion fruit cake, perfect for an afternoon tea party. Don't be put off by the long ingredients list – it really is very simple.

Serves 12
Preparation time:
  25 minutes + cooling
Baking time:
  4–4½ hours

250 g (9 oz) **plain flour**
¼ teaspoon **salt**
2 teaspoons **baking powder**
1 teaspoon **mixed spice**
½ teaspoon **ground cinnamon**
½ teaspoon **ground nutmeg**
225 g (8 oz) **currants**
225 g (8 oz) **sultanas**
225 g (8 oz) **raisins**
110 g (4 oz) **glacé cherries**
225 g (8 oz) soft **margarine**
225 g (8 oz) **light brown soft sugar**
5 **eggs**
1 tablespoon **black treacle**
110 g (4 oz) **mixed peel**
grated zest of 1 **lemon**
grated zest of 1 **orange**
1 tablespoon **lemon juice**
2 tablespoons **sherry**
60 g (2 oz) **ground almonds**
60 g (2 oz) **blanched almonds**, chopped

Preheat the oven to 150°C/300°F/Gas Mark 2. Grease a 20 cm (8 inch) square or a 23 cm (9 inch) round cake tin and line with doubled non-stick baking parchment or greased greaseproof paper. Place a double thickness of brown paper around the outside of the tin to protect the sides of the cake during cooking.

Sieve the flour with the salt, baking powder and spices. Wash the dried fruit and quarter and wash the glacé cherries. Dry thoroughly.

Place all the ingredients in a mixing bowl and beat together until well blended. Place in the prepared tin and hollow out the centre a little.

Bake for 1 hour and then reduce the oven temperature to 140°C/275°F/Gas Mark 1 and continue to cook for a further 3–3½ hours or until the cake is firm to the touch and beginning to shrink slightly from the sides of the tin. It may be necessary to place a sheet of foil or greaseproof paper over the cake to prevent it over-browning.

Leave in the tin until cold and then turn out. Wrap in greaseproof paper and foil, store to mature the cake, then ice or use as desired.

Lemon cake

There are many WI variations on the classic lemon cake, or lemon drizzle cake as it is commonly known.

Serves 8
Preparation time:
  20 minutes + cooling
Baking time:
  50–60 minutes

175 g (6 oz) soft **margarine**
175 g (6 oz) **caster sugar**
2 **eggs**, lightly beaten
4 tablespoons **milk**
175 g (6 oz) **self-raising
  flour**, sieved
finely grated zest and juice
  of 1 large **lemon**
1 tablespoon **icing sugar**

Preheat the oven to 180°C/350°F/Gas Mark 4. Lightly grease a 900 g (2 lb) loaf tin and line with non-stick baking parchment or greased greaseproof paper.

Cream the margarine and caster sugar together until light and creamy and then gradually beat in the eggs together with the milk.

Lightly fold in the sieved flour and lemon zest. Place in the prepared tin and smooth the top.

Bake for 50–60 minutes or until the cake is golden brown, firm to the touch and beginning to shrink from the sides of the tin.

Mix the lemon juice with the icing sugar and pour over the cake as soon as it has been taken out of the oven.

Allow the glaze to set, remove the cake from the tin and place on a wire rack to cool.

Note The Lancashire WI's 'Luscious Lemon Cake' (taken from the *Lancashire Cook Book*'s Diamond Jubilee edition) advises pricking the cake all over with a fork while still warm. The icing then seeps into the cake to ensure it's really moist.

Strawberry jelly cake

Quintessentially British, strawberries and cream make the perfect addition to afternoon tea. Layer with buttery crumbs for a decadent dessert.

Serves 6
Preparation time:
1 hour + chilling
Cooking time:
10–15 minutes

110 g (4 oz) **butter**, softened
60 g (2 oz) **demerara sugar**
60 g (2 oz) **walnuts**, finely
  chopped
110 g (4 oz) **plain flour**
2 x 12 g sachets powdered
  gelatine
450 g (1 lb) **strawberries**,
  hulled and thickly sliced
1 teaspoon **lemon juice**
175 g (6 oz) **caster sugar**
300 ml (10 fl oz) **double**
  cream

Preheat the oven to 200°C/400°F/Gas Mark 6. Rub the butter, demerara sugar, walnuts and flour together. Scatter this mixture over a shallow tin and bake for 10–15 minutes. Leave to cool and then crumble into a mixing bowl.

Place the gelatine in a small bowl with 4 tablespoons of water and leave to soften for a few minutes.

Mash a quarter of the strawberries in a small saucepan and add the lemon juice and caster sugar. Bring this mixture to the boil, take off the heat, add the softened gelatine and stir until completely dissolved.

Put a little of this mixture through a strainer into the base of a 1.2 litre (2 pint) jelly mould and chill for 15–20 minutes to set.

Whip the cream until it just holds its shape and then fold in the remaining sliced strawberries.

When the remaining gelatine mixture is cold and on the point of setting, fold it into the strawberries and cream. Immediately fill the mould with layers of the strawberry mixture and crumbs, starting with strawberry and ending with crumbs, gently pressing the crumbs into the cream mixture after each addition. Chill for 2–3 hours to set.

To serve, turn out of the mould. Dip the mould briefly in hot (but not boiling) water, loosen the edge of the cake with a fingertip, cover the mould with a plate, turn upside down and then jerk the plate and mould to release the jelly.

Tip If you like, decorate up to 1 hour before needed. Whip 150 ml (5 fl oz) of whipping or double cream, just until it holds its shape, then pipe it around the base of the cake. Arrange a large sliced strawberry around the cream.

Gâteau St Georges

This is a glamorous chocolate variation of lemon meringue pie – utterly irresistible.

Serves 8
Preparation time:
   40 minutes + cooling
Baking time:
   40–50 minutes

Génoise sponge cake mixture (see page 108)
110 g (4 oz) **dark chocolate** (70% cocoa solids), broken into pieces
3 **eggs**, separated
60 g (2 oz) **butter**, softened
2 teaspoons **rum**
110 g (4 oz) **caster sugar**
cocoa powder, to decorate

Preheat the oven to 180°C/350°F/Gas Mark 4. Grease a 20–23 cm (8–9 inch) sponge flan tin, base line with a round of non-stick baking parchment and grease again.

Pour the Génoise cake mixture into the tin and bake for 20–30 minutes until the cake starts to shrink away from the sides of the tin. Turn out and leave to cool.

Place the chocolate and 1 tablespoon of water in a bowl and melt over a pan of simmering water. When completely melted, remove from the heat.

Beat the egg yolks, one at a time, into the chocolate with the butter and the rum. When the butter is completely absorbed, pour the mixture on to the sponge. Leave to set. Preheat the oven to 160°C/325°F/Gas Mark 3.

Whisk the egg whites in a large clean bowl until stiff peaks form. Add the caster sugar a teaspoon at a time, whisking until all the sugar has been absorbed and you have a glossy meringue.

Swirl the meringue on to the set chocolate and cook until set on the outside, about 20 minutes. It need not dry out, but must be firmly set on top. Serve cold, decorated with a sprinkling of cocoa powder.

Tips A wooden spoon is too thick for any folding operation. The thin edge of a metal spoon cuts through mixtures without breaking down the airy texture.

To save time, or if you don't have a sponge flan tin, make this with a ready-bought sponge flan ring.

Instead of adding the rum to the chocolate mixture, try drizzling up to 2 tablespoons over the sponge flan.

Eccles cakes

Named after the English town of Eccles, these delicious flat pastries also go by the name of squashed fly cakes due to their packed filling of currants.

Makes 10
Preparation time:
   40 minutes + 1 hour
   chilling + cooling
Cooking time:
   15 minutes

175 g (6 oz) **butter**
225 g (8 oz) **plain flour**
a pinch of **salt**
1 **egg white**
caster sugar, for sprinkling

Filling
60 g (2 oz) **demerara sugar**
60 g (2 oz) **butter**, softened
110 g (4 oz) **currants**
60 g (2 oz) **mixed peel**, finely
   chopped
¼ teaspoon **mixed spice**

To make the pastry, wrap the butter in foil and place it in the freezer for 30 minutes.

Sift the flour and salt into a bowl. Holding the butter with the foil, dip it into the flour and then grate it into the bowl using a coarse grater placed over the flour. Keep dipping the butter into the flour to make it easier to grate.

Using a palette knife, start to cut the butter into the flour until the mixture is crumbly. Add enough cold water (4–4½ tablespoons) to form a dough that leaves the bowl clean, place it in a polythene bag and chill for 30 minutes.

Meanwhile, for the filling, mix the sugar, butter, currants, peel and spice together in a bowl. Preheat the oven to 220°C/425°F/ Gas Mark 7.

Roll out the pastry on a lightly floured surface to 4 mm (¼ inch) thick. Cut out 10 rounds using a 10 cm (4 inch) cutter, re-rolling the trimmings as necessary.

Place a teaspoonful of the mixture in the centre of each round pastry, wet the edges with water and pull them together to seal in the middle. Turn each round over and flatten with the rolling pin until the fruit is just visible or the rounds are about 7.5 cm (3 inches) in diameter. Make three cuts in the centre of each round.

Place on a greased baking tray, brush with the egg white and sprinkle with caster sugar. Bake for about 15 minutes until golden. Cool on a wire rack.

Old-fashioned treacle tart

For those with a sweet tooth, there can be few afternoon tea pastries to rival the treacle tart. Fruit rind and spice add a touch of luxury.

Serves 6
Preparation time:
  20 minutes +
  30 minutes chilling
Baking time:
  25–30 minutes

25 g (1 oz) **butter**
25 g (1 oz) **white vegetable fat**
110 g (4 oz) **plain flour**
a pinch of **salt**
clotted cream, to serve

Filling
8 tablespoons **golden syrup**
2 tablespoons **black treacle**
50 g (1¾ oz) **raisins**
25 g (1 oz) **mixed peel**
25 g (1 oz) **walnuts**, roughly chopped
finely grated zest of ½ **lemon**
finely grated zest of ½ **orange**
a good pinch of ground **allspice**
50 g (1¾ oz) fresh **breadcrumbs**

Preheat the oven to 200°C/400°F/Gas Mark 6.

Make the pastry by rubbing the butter and vegetable fat into the flour until the mixture resembles breadcrumbs. Add the salt and enough cold water to create a dough (4–5 teaspoons). Wrap in cling film and chill for 30 minutes.

Roll the pastry out fairly thinly on a lightly floured surface and use to line a 20 cm (8 inch) deep pie plate or flan dish. Prick the bottom of the pastry case with a fork, line with non-stick baking parchment or greaseproof paper, fill with baking beans and bake blind for 10 minutes. Remove the beans and paper and bake for a further 5 minutes to dry and crisp the base. Reduce the oven temperature to 180°C/350°F/Gas Mark 4.

Gently warm the syrup and treacle together.

Scatter the raisins, peel and walnuts into the pastry case and sprinkle with the fruit zest and allspice, reserving a little zest for decoration. Pour over the warmed syrup and treacle and sprinkle with the breadcrumbs, leaving for a few minutes to settle and soak in.

Bake for 25–30 minutes or until the filling is firm and the pastry lightly browned. Serve warm or cold with spoonfuls of clotted cream and decorated with the reserved fruit zest.

Battenburg cake

This chequered sponge is said to have first been baked to celebrate Prince Louis of Battenburg's marriage to Princess Victoria in 1884.

Serves 6
Preparation time:
20 minutes +
1–2 hours setting +
cooling
Baking time:
25–30 minutes

225 g (8 oz) **butter** or
  margarine, softened
225 g (8 oz) **caster sugar**
4 **eggs**
225 g (8 oz) **self-raising flour**
½ teaspoon **baking powder**
red **food colouring**
raspberry or **apricot jam**
225 g (8 oz) **marzipan**
icing sugar, for dusting

Preheat the oven to 180°C/350°F/Gas Mark 4. Grease two 900 g (2 lb) loaf tins and base line with non-stick baking parchment or greased greaseproof paper.

Cream the butter or margarine and sugar together and beat in the eggs. Sieve the flour and baking powder together, fold into the mixture and mix to a dropping consistency, adding a little hot water if necessary.

Put half the mixture into one of the prepared tins. Add a couple of drops of red food colouring to the remaining mixture to make it pale pink and put it into the second tin.

Bake for 25–30 minutes until a skewer inserted in the centre comes out clean. Allow to cool in the tin for a few minutes and then turn out on to a wire rack.

When cold, trim the cakes and cut two lengths from each one, each approximately 3 cm (1½ inches) square. Spread the pieces with jam and stick the four lengths together, the colours alternating. Wrap in greaseproof paper very tightly and leave for an hour or two.

Spread the outside of the cake with jam. Roll out the marzipan in a little icing sugar to an oblong the same width as the cake and long enough to wrap around.

Place the cake on the marzipan and wrap it around the cake, pressing it neatly and arranging the join in one lower corner. If you wish, crimp the edge and mark the top with a criss-cross pattern. Wrap the cake in paper again and keep for 3–4 hours in a cool place before eating.

Scones

Jam then cream? Or cream then jam? The age-old debate goes back and forth as scones continue to take centre stage at any good afternoon tea.

Makes 8–10
Preparation time:
  10 minutes + cooling
Baking time:
  12–15 minutes

225 g (8 oz) **plain flour**
¼ teaspoon **salt**
1 teaspoon **cream of tartar**
½ teaspoon **bicarbonate of soda**
60 g (2 oz) **butter**, diced
150 ml (5 fl oz) **milk** or **buttermilk**
1 **egg**, beaten, or **milk**, to glaze

Preheat the oven to 230°C/450°F/Gas Mark 8. Either grease a baking tray or dredge it liberally with flour.

Sift the flour, salt, cream of tartar and bicarbonate of soda into a bowl. Add the butter and rub in until the mixture resembles fine breadcrumbs.

Add enough milk or buttermilk to mix to a fairly soft dough using a palette knife or spatula.

Turn out on to a lightly floured surface and gently flatten the dough out to 2–2.5 cm (¾–1 inch) thick. Using a well-floured 4–5 cm (1½–2 inch) plain or fluted cutter, or an upturned glass, stamp out the scones.

Re-roll the trimmings to cut out more scones and place on the baking tray. Either brush the tops with the beaten egg or milk, or dredge lightly with flour.

Bake for 12–15 minutes until well risen, golden brown and just firm. Remove to a wire rack and leave to cool.

Tip Whatever your topping preference, these are best served warm on the day they are made – the perfect bridge between piles of sandwiches and cake. However, they reheat well and freeze for up to 3 months.

Variations **Fruit** – add 50 g (1¾ oz) of currants, sultanas, raisins or cut mixed peel to the dry ingredients.

Cheese – add a pinch of dried mustard and 40–50 g (1½–1¾ oz) of finely grated mature Cheddar cheese or 1–2 level tablespoons of grated Parmesan cheese to the dry ingredients.

Golden flapjacks

This delicious recipe, with a hint of coconut, hails from Worcestershire – sure proof that everyone has their own secret flapjack recipe.

Serves 6–8
Preparation time:
  20 minutes + cooling
Baking time:
  20 minutes

140 g (5 oz) **butter**
140 g (5 oz) **demerara sugar**
140 g (5 oz) **rolled oats**
3 drops **vanilla extract**
2 tablespoons **desiccated coconut**

Preheat the oven to 190°C/375°F/Gas Mark 5. Lightly grease a 30 × 20 cm (12 × 8 inch) Swiss roll tin.

Melt the butter over a low heat in a saucepan. Add the sugar, oats and vanilla extract. Mix well, add the coconut and mix again.

Turn out into the prepared tin and spread out with a fork, pressing down firmly.

Bake for 20 minutes or until golden brown. Cut into fingers while in the tin and leave to cool and crisp.

Note This recipe is from *The WI Recipe Book*, 1965 – a compilation of the best regional recipes sent in by WI members and described in the foreword as a 'unique collection of ways with food'.

Hot cross buns

A sticky hot cross bun is the ultimate Easter treat but can be enjoyed all year round. Eat them plain, toasted or spread with jam.

Makes 24
Preparation time:
  20 minutes + 2 hours rising + cooling
Baking time:
  15 minutes

900 g (2 lb) **strong white bread flour**

1 teaspoon **salt**

1–2 teaspoons **mixed spice**

4 teaspoons **fast action dried yeast**

110 g (4 oz) **caster sugar**, plus 2 level tablespoons for the glaze

110 g (4 oz) **butter**, diced

110 g (4 oz) **sultanas**

about 425 ml (15 fl oz) half and half warm **milk** and **water**

110 g (4 oz) **plain flour**

Place the bread flour, salt, mixed spice, yeast and sugar in a large bowl and mix together. Rub in the butter until the mixture resembles breadcrumbs and then add the sultanas.

Add the milk and water and mix to form a soft dough. Knead on a lightly floured surface for about 10 minutes until the dough is smooth and elastic.

Place in a clean, lightly oiled bowl, cover with oiled cling film or a clean tea towel and set aside in a warm place to rise for about 1½ hours or until doubled in size. Knead again for 2–3 minutes.

Divide the dough into 24 pieces, knead each piece until smooth and shape into buns. Place on lightly greased baking trays, allowing room for the buns to rise.

Cover with oiled cling film and leave in a warm place until doubled in size – about 30 minutes. Preheat the oven to 220°C/425°F/Gas Mark 7.

Mix the plain flour to a smooth paste with 8 tablespoons of water and spoon into a piping bag fitted with an 8 mm (⅜ inch) plain nozzle. Pipe crosses over the tops of the buns. Bake for 15 minutes or until brown and cooked.

While the buns are cooking, dissolve the 2 level tablespoons of sugar in 2 tablespoons of water. Bring to the boil and brush over the buns while still hot. Cool on a wire rack.

Pikelets

A warm pikelet (or crumpet) oozing with butter is the epitome of afternoon tea. Add jam with the butter or serve with syrup.

Makes 24–28
Preparation time:
  10 minutes +
  1½ hours rising
Cooking time:
  30 minutes

450 g (1 lb) **strong white bread flour**
¼ teaspoon **bicarbonate of soda**
1 teaspoon **caster sugar**
½ teaspoon **salt**
1½ teaspoons **fast action dried yeast**
600 ml (20 fl oz) half and half warm **milk** and **water**
butter, for greasing

Stir the flour, bicarbonate of soda, sugar, salt and yeast together in a large mixing bowl.

Gradually add the milk and water to make a smooth batter. Beat for a couple of minutes with a balloon whisk.

Cover with oiled cling film or a clean, damp tea towel, and leave to rise for up to 1½ hours in a warm place until the mixture is light and frothy.

Beat the batter again for about 1 minute.

Grease a griddle pan or heavy-based frying pan and heat. Drop tablespoons of the batter on to the griddle and cook for a couple of minutes. When the tops are covered in holes, turn over. Continue to cook for another 30 seconds; the pikelets should be golden brown one side and pale brown the other.

Continue to cook until all the batter has been used up. Serve straight away or cool on a wire rack.

Tip If you have them, use lightly greased 7.5 cm (3 inch) baking rings on the pan to create a nice neat shape for the pikelet. You can also create your own baking rings from lightly greased, washed tin cans with the labels, tops and bottoms removed.

Note This recipe is taken from the *National Federation of Women's Institutes' Yeast Cookery Book*, 1952, published with technical advice from the Ministry of Food following 'an increased interest in home baking and Yeast Cookery' that convinced the WI Committee that the publication would 'fill a gap in the ranks of cookery books' at that time.

Queen cakes

For a regal touch to afternoon tea, try these sweet and light queen cakes. Quick and easy to make, they taste delicious.

Makes 10–12
Preparation time:
  15 minutes
Baking time:
  15–20 minutes

110 g (4 oz) soft **margarine**
110 g (4 oz) **caster sugar**,
  plus extra for sprinkling
2 **eggs**, beaten
110 g (4 oz) **self-raising
  flour**, sieved
a little **milk**, if necessary
60 g (2 oz) **dried fruit**

Preheat the oven to 180°C/350°F/Gas Mark 4. Grease a 12-hole bun or mini bundt tin.

Cream the margarine and sugar together. Add the eggs a little at a time, beating well.

Fold the flour into the mixture with a little milk, if necessary, to give a soft dropping consistency. Add the fruit and mix well.

Place spoonfuls of the mixture into the prepared tin. Bake for 15–20 minutes until firm to the touch and golden brown. Turn out on a wire rack to cool and sprinkle with a little extra caster sugar.

Note The recipe is taken from the *Berkshire WI Cookery Book* (1958), a collection of 'cherished recipes', as described by Doris Cuming in the book's foreword: 'It may be thought that, in the future, pre-packed and prepared food will replace the individuality of home cooking. Although these commodities may have to take their place in the running of a busy home and cannot be ignored, tradition and craft have too strong a hold on the memory to be lost easily; by fostering good standards of home cooking, one has some means of comparison and discrimination.'

Variations Use 60 g (2 oz) of washed, chopped glacé cherries instead of the dried fruit, or replace 1 tablespoon of flour with 1 tablespoon of cocoa powder.

Bakewell tart

Hailing from the town of Bakewell in Derbyshire, this tart is as popular now as it was when it first appeared in the early 1800s.

Serves 6–8
Preparation time:
30 minutes +
30 minutes chilling
Baking time:
45–50 minutes

icing sugar, for dusting

For the pastry
80 g (3 oz) **butter** or
   margarine
225 g (8 oz) **plain flour**
a pinch of **salt**
1 **egg**, beaten

For the filling
60 g (2 oz) **butter**, softened
80 g (3 oz) **caster sugar**
2 large **eggs**
80 g (3 oz) **ground almonds**
80 g (3 oz) **cake** or **bread**,
   crumbled
grated zest and juice of
   ½ **lemon**
milk, if necessary
2 tablespoons **red jam**

To make the pastry, rub the butter or margarine into the flour and salt until the mixture resembles breadcrumbs. Add the egg and enough cold water to form a dough. Wrap in cling film and chill for 30 minutes. Preheat the oven to 190°C/375°F/Gas Mark 5.

Roll out the pastry thinly on a lightly floured surface. Line an 18 cm (7 inch) pie or flan dish with the pastry, prick the base, line with non-stick baking parchment and fill with baking beans.

Bake blind for 15 minutes and then remove the baking beans and parchment and return to the oven for a further 5 minutes until dry and crisp. Remove from the oven and allow to cool. Reduce the oven temperature to 180°C/350°F/Gas Mark 4.

Cream the butter and sugar together and beat in the eggs with the ground almonds, cake or breadcrumbs and lemon zest and juice. Add a little milk if necessary to achieve the right consistency.

Spread the pastry base with the jam. Spread the almond mixture over the jam and bake for 25–30 minutes. Cool and then dust with icing sugar just before serving.

Custard tart

Wobbly baked custard and a dusting of nutmeg set in a sweet pastry crust makes this tart a true British classic.

Serves 4–6
Preparation time:
 20 minutes
Baking time:
 45 minutes

175 g (6 oz) **sweet pastry**
cornflour, for dusting
275 ml (10 fl oz) **full-fat milk**
 or **single cream**
1 large **egg**, plus 2 extra
 egg yolks
15 g (½ oz) **caster sugar**
a little grated **nutmeg**

Preheat the oven to 200°C/400°F/Gas Mark 6.

Roll out the pastry as thinly as possible on a surface dusted with cornflour. Lift the pastry on to the rolling pin and use to line an 18 cm (7 inch) loose-bottomed flan tin.

Using a little ball of pastry as a pusher, press out all the air trapped between the pastry and the tin. Prick the pastry and press again. Cover the pastry with non-stick baking parchment paper and fill with baking beans. Bake blind on a baking tray for about 15 minutes.

Meanwhile, make the custard. Bring the milk or cream to the boil and whisk the egg and egg yolks with the sugar. Slowly pour the boiling milk or cream into the egg mixture, whisking all the time. Whisk for another few minutes, by which time the flan case should be cooked. Pour the custard into a jug.

Remove the tin from the oven and remove the paper and baking beans. Lower the oven temperature to 150°C/300°F/Gas Mark 2. Replace the tin in the oven.

Pull the oven rack with the flan case a little way out of the oven and gently pour the custard into the case. Sprinkle with a little grated nutmeg. Ease the oven rack gently back into the oven and cook the tart for about 30 minutes until set.

Hereford curd cake

This is a cross between a cheesecake and a tart. Traditionally made by straining soured milk for 24 hours, this is made using natural yogurt.

Serves 8
Preparation time:
  30 minutes + draining
  + 30 minutes chilling
Baking time:
  30 minutes

For the curd
500 g (1 lb 2 oz) **natural set yogurt**
60 g (2 oz) **butter,** softened
1 **egg,** beaten
1 tablespoon **brandy**
a little grated **lemon zest**
1 tablespoon **currants**
25 g (1 oz) **caster sugar**
a pinch of **salt**
1 tablespoon **milk**
a little grated **nutmeg**

For the short pastry
60 g (2 oz) **butter** or **margarine**
140 g (5 oz) **plain flour**
a pinch of **salt**

Line a large sieve with muslin and spoon the yogurt into it. Place over a bowl and allow it to drain in the fridge for a couple of hours.

Make the pastry by rubbing the butter or margarine into the flour until the mixture resembles breadcrumbs. Add the salt and enough cold water to form a dough. Cover with cling film and chill in the fridge for 30 minutes.

Remove the curd from the muslin and mix with the butter. Add all the remaining ingredients except the grated nutmeg. Preheat the oven to 190°C/375°F/Gas Mark 5.

Roll out the pastry and use to line a 20 cm (8 inch) sandwich tin or fluted flan tin. Pour the curd mixture into the pastry case and sprinkle a little grated nutmeg over the top.

Bake for about 30 minutes until the curd mixture is set and the pastry is cooked, reducing the oven temperature to 180°C/350°F/Gas Mark 4 for the final 10 minutes.

Guernsey Gâche

Afternoon tea would be nothing on the island of Guernsey without a slab of this fruity loaf, best served toasted with lashings of Guernsey butter.

Serves 20
Preparation time:
  20 minutes + proving
Baking time:
  70–75 minutes

450 g (1 lb) **butter**, Guernsey
  if possible
675 g (1 lb 8 oz) **plain flour**
2 tablespoons **caster sugar**
4 teaspoons **fast action**
  dried yeast
a pinch of **salt**
½ teaspoon **grated nutmeg**
450 g (1 lb) **currants** or
  sultanas
110 g (4 oz) **mixed peel**
200 ml (7 fl oz) half and half
  warm **water** and **milk**

Rub the butter into the flour until the mixture resembles breadcrumbs. Add the sugar, yeast, salt, nutmeg, fruit and peel.

Make a well in the centre of the dry ingredients and gradually add enough water and milk to mix to a soft dough that leaves the bowl and your hands clean.

Knead well on an unfloured surface, place back in the bowl and cover with a thick cloth. Place in a warm place for 1½–2 hours to rise.

Preheat the oven to 180°C/350°F/Gas Mark 4. Grease a 20 cm (8 inch) deep round cake tin.

Knead the mixture again and then place in the prepared tin. Bake for 70–75 minutes until golden brown.

Fat rascals

These scones cum rock-cakes were first made in Elizabethan times. Today, a well-known Yorkshire tea room makes about 350,000 annually.

Makes 12
Preparation time:
   15 minutes + cooling
Baking time:
   12–15 minutes

110 g (4 oz) **butter**
225 g (8 oz) **self-raising flour**
a pinch of **salt**
25 g (1 oz) **caster sugar**
60 g (2 oz) **currants**
4–6 tablespoons **milk**

Preheat the oven to 190°C/375°F/Gas Mark 5. Lightly grease a baking tray.

Rub the butter into the flour and salt. Add the sugar and currants and mix with enough milk to form a soft dough.

Drop spoonfuls of the mixture on to the baking tray or roll out on a lightly floured surface to 1 cm (½ inch) thick and cut into rounds with a 5 cm (2 inch) cutter, if preferred.

Bake on the second shelf from the top for 12–15 minutes. Cool on a wire rack.

Tip If you like a sweeter cake, sprinkle with some crushed sugar lumps before baking.

Sally Lunns

Wander into any of Bath's picturesque tea shops and you'll find the Sally Lunn – a brioche-like bread traditionally served with butter or cream.

Makes 1
Preparation time:
  20 minutes + proving
Baking time:
  20 minutes

75 ml (3 fl oz) **milk**
35 g (1¼ oz) **butter**
1 **egg**, lightly beaten
450 g (1 lb) **strong plain flour**
1½ teaspoons **fast action dried yeast**
½ teaspoon **salt**
80 g (3 oz) **caster sugar**

Grease a 18 cm (7 inch) round cake tin.

Heat the milk and 150 ml (5 fl oz) of water in a small saucepan until lukewarm. Add the butter and stir to melt. Cool slightly until it is tepid. Add the egg.

Sieve the flour into a bowl. Stir in the yeast, salt and sugar. Make a well in the middle and pour in the liquid, mixing to form a soft dough.

Turn out on to a lightly floured surface and knead for about 8 minutes until smooth and elastic. Place in the prepared tin, cover and set aside in a warm place to rise for about 1 hour. Preheat the oven to 220°C/425°F/Gas Mark 7.

Bake for about 20 minutes until golden brown. Transfer to a wire rack to cool.

Dorset apple cake

From the WI Dorset Federation book – *Cookery Recipes and Household Hints* – this is still the pride of the county. Serve warm with cream.

Serves 8
Preparation time:
  15 minutes + cooling
Baking time:
  45 minutes

450 g (1 lb) **plain flour**
110 g (4 oz) **golden caster sugar**
3 teaspoons **baking powder**
225 g (8 oz) **butter**, diced
450 g (1 lb) **cooking apples**, peeled and cored
2 **eggs**, lightly beaten
60 ml (2 fl oz) **milk**

Preheat the oven to 180°C/350°F/Gas Mark 4. Grease a 23 cm (9 inch) cake tin and line with non-stick baking parchment or greased greaseproof paper.

Mix the flour, sugar and baking powder together in a large bowl. Add the butter and rub in to resemble breadcrumbs.

Grate the apples into the mixture and add the eggs and milk. Mix until combined. Spoon into the prepared tin, levelling the surface, and bake for 45 minutes until golden brown and a skewer inserted in the centre comes out clean.

Allow to cool in the tin for 10 minutes before turning out.

Tip Sprinkling the surface with demerara sugar before baking gives a lovely crunchy top.

Devonshire splits

Also known as Devonshire buns or Chudleighs, these date back to the 19th century and are traditionally served with treacle or jam and clotted cream.

Makes 16
Preparation time:
  20 minutes + rising
Baking time:
  15–20 minutes

450 g (1 lb) **plain flour**
½ teaspoon **salt**
1 teaspoon **caster sugar**
7 g sachet **fast action dried yeast**
300 ml (10 fl oz) warm **skimmed milk**
60 g (2 oz) **butter**, melted

Syrup
110 g (4 oz) **caster sugar**
75 ml (3 fl oz) **milk**

To serve
jam
clotted cream
icing sugar, sifted

Grease and flour two baking trays. Sift the flour and salt into a mixing bowl and stir in the sugar and yeast. Add the milk and melted butter and mix to form a soft dough.

Turn out on to a lightly floured surface and knead for 10 minutes. Put into a floured bowl, cover with a clean damp tea towel or oiled cling film and set aside in a warm place until doubled in size (about 30 minutes). Preheat the oven to 200°C/400°F/Gas Mark 6.

Turn out the dough and divide into 16 equal portions. Knead into small balls with the palm of the hand. Place on the prepared baking trays, cover with a tea towel and set aside for 10–15 minutes or until doubled in size. Bake for 15–20 minutes until golden brown.

Heat the sugar and milk together until the sugar has dissolved and brush the hot cooked buns with this syrupy mixture to make them soft and sticky.

When cold, split, fill with jam and Devonshire clotted cream and dust with a little icing sugar.

Lincolnshire plum bun

Plum is an old English word for mixed fruit. This is a delicious moist tea loaf, ideally served cut into thin slices and buttered.

**Makes 2 x 2 lb loaves
or 1 x 2 lb loaf +
6 mini loaves
Preparation time:
20 minutes
Baking time:
50 minutes–1½ hours**

150 g (5½ oz) **butter** or
    margarine, softened
300 g (10½ oz) **light
    muscovado sugar**
1 **egg**, lightly beaten
1 tablespoon **rum** (optional)
450 g (1 lb) **self-raising flour**
1 teaspoon **mixed spice**
250 g (9 oz) **currants**
250 g (9 oz) **sultanas**
40 g (1½ oz) chopped **mixed
    peel**
40 g (1½ oz) **glacé cherries**
150 ml (5 fl oz) **milk** or **cold
    tea**

Preheat the oven to 150°C/300°F/Gas Mark 2. Grease two 900 g (2 lb) loaf tins and line with non-stick baking parchment or greased greaseproof paper. Alternatively, prepare one 900 g (2 lb) tin and six mini 200 ml (7 fl oz) loaf tins.

Cream the butter or margarine and sugar together and mix in the egg and rum, if using.

Fold in the flour and then the remaining ingredients.

Divide the mixture between the prepared tins and bake for 1¼–1½ hours for the larger tins and 50–60 minutes for the mini ones. They are done when they are golden brown and a skewer inserted into the centre comes out clean.

Tip This will keep for up to a fortnight in an airtight tin.

Wiltshire lardy cake

Enriched with sugar and spices and studded with fruit, this rich and gooey tea bread is not for the faint-hearted. Best enjoyed warm with a cup of tea.

Serves 8–10
Preparation time:
 30 minutes + rising
Baking time:
 25–30 minutes

450 g (1 lb) **strong white bread flour**
½ teaspoon **salt**
½ teaspoon **mixed spice**
1½ teaspoons **fast action dried yeast**
110 g (4 oz) **caster sugar**
300 ml (10 fl oz) warm **milk**

To finish
110 g (4 oz) **lard** or **white vegetable fat**
110 g (4 oz) **caster sugar**, plus 2 tablespoons for topping
110 g (4 oz) mixed **dried fruit**

Warm the flour, salt and spice by heating it in the microwave for a few seconds or popping it into a warm oven for a few minutes.

Stir in the yeast and sugar and then gradually add enough warm milk to mix to a soft but not sticky dough.

Knead well on a lightly floured surface for about 10 minutes until the dough is smooth and elastic. Place in a clean bowl and cover with a damp tea towel or greased cling film. Set aside in a warm place until doubled in size – about 1 hour.

Knead the dough again for a few minutes and then roll out on a well floured board to a rectangle about 4 mm (¼ inch) thick. Spread on half the lard, sugar and fruit. Fold in three, folding the bottom third up and the top third down, turn the mixture 90 degrees to the left and roll out again. Cover with the rest of the lard, sugar and fruit and fold in three again.

Roll out to a 2.5 cm (1 inch) thick oblong that will fit in a greased 25 x 20 cm (10 x 8 inch) roasting tin. Place the dough in the tin, cover with greased cling film and stand in a warm place until well risen (30–45 minutes). Preheat the oven to 220°C/425°F/Gas Mark 7.

Score the top of the dough in a criss-cross pattern with a knife. Dissolve the remaining 2 tablespoons of sugar in 2 tablespoons of hot water and brush the top of the cake.

Bake for 25–30 minutes until well risen and golden brown. Check after 20 minutes and cover loosely with foil if the top seems to be browning too much.

Tips The lard can be replaced with butter for a healthier version.

Rather than brushing the cake with a sugar solution before baking, you could just sprinkle the sugar over the top of the cake when it comes out of the oven.

Chocolate caramel slices

Traditional biscuit bases covered with gooey delicious caramel and topped with melted chocolate. Rich but fabulous.

Makes 18
Preparation time:
 30 minutes + cooling
Baking time:
 25 minutes

For the base
110 g (4 oz) **butter** or
 margarine
140 g (5 oz) **plain flour**
a pinch of **salt**
60 g (2 oz) **caster sugar**

Filling
110 g (4 oz) **margarine**
2 tablespoons **golden syrup**
110 g (4 oz) **light brown soft**
 sugar
1 small tin **condensed milk**
a few drops of **vanilla**
 extract

Topping
110 g (4 oz) **plain chocolate**
 (70% cocoa solids),
 broken into pieces

Preheat the oven to 160°C/325°F/Gas Mark 3. Grease an 18 cm (7 inch) square loose-bottomed tin.

For the base, rub the butter or margarine into the flour, salt and sugar. Knead into a ball and then press out evenly into the prepared tin. Bake for 25 minutes. Leave to cool before adding the filling and topping.

For the filling, slowly melt the margarine, syrup, sugar and condensed milk together, stirring continuously. Bring to the boil and, still stirring, simmer gently for exactly 7 minutes.

Add the vanilla extract, pour on to the base and leave to cool.

For the topping, melt the chocolate gently in a bowl over a pan of simmering water. Beat until it is smooth.

Spread the chocolate evenly over the filling. When set, cut into nine squares and then cut each square in half again to make 18 slices.

Tips If you don't have a loose-bottomed tin, line the tin with non-stick baking parchment, snipping into the corners of the paper so it lines the bottom and sides. This makes it easier to remove the slices.

It is easier to cut this into slices if you make it the day before and chill in the fridge.

Butterfly cakes

An old-fashioned favourite loved by all and fun to make with children. Decorate with ready-made icing and sweets to take into school fêtes.

Makes 12
Preparation time:
  30 minutes + cooling
Cooking time:
  15–18 minutes

110 g (4 oz) soft **margarine**
110 g (4 oz) **caster sugar**
110 g (4 oz) **self-raising flour**
½ teaspoon **baking powder**
2 **eggs**
1 teaspoon **vanilla essence**

Butter cream frosting
110 g (4 oz) **butter**, softened
225 g (8 oz) **icing sugar**,
  sifted, plus extra to
  decorate
½ teaspoon **vanilla essence**
1–2 teaspoons **milk**

Preheat the oven to 180°C/350°F/Gas Mark 4. Line a 12-hole bun tin with paper cake cases.

Place the margarine, sugar, flour and baking powder in a mixing bowl, add the eggs and vanilla essence and beat until smooth with a wooden spoon or electric mixer.

Spoon into the cake cases, level the tops and bake for 15–18 minutes until well risen and golden brown and the tops spring back when pressed lightly with a fingertip. Leave the cakes to cool a little in the tin then transfer to a wire rack.

To make the frosting, beat the butter and half the icing sugar in a bowl until smooth. Add the remaining icing sugar and the vanilla essence and beat until soft and smooth, adding milk as needed.

Cut a small circle from the top of each cake using a teaspoon. Pipe or spoon butter cream into the centre of the cakes. Cut the small cake circles in half and press into the butter cream at angles to resemble wings. Dust lightly with a little extra sifted icing sugar.

Éclairs

Everyone's favourite – light, crisp pastry fingers filled with cream and iced with chocolate.

Makes 12
Preparation time:
 45 minutes + cooling
Baking time:
 30–35 minutes

275 ml (10 fl oz) **whipping cream**
25 g (1 oz) **icing sugar**
75 g (2¾ oz) **plain chocolate** (70% cocoa solids), broken into pieces
15 g (½ oz) **butter**
60 g (2 oz) **icing sugar**, sifted

Choux pastry
60 g (2 oz) **butter,** diced
70 g (2½ oz) **strong white flour**
1 teaspoon **caster sugar**
2 **eggs**, beaten

Preheat the oven to 200°C/400°F/Gas Mark 6. Arrange two shelves in the top half of the oven if it isn't fan assisted. Grease and flour two baking trays.

To make the choux pastry, put 150 ml (5 fl oz) of cold water and the butter in a saucepan. Place over a medium heat until the butter has melted and it all comes to the boil. Meanwhile, sieve the flour on to a sheet of baking parchment that has been folded in half.

Remove the butter water from the heat and 'shoot' the flour into the mixture with the sugar. Beat vigorously with a wooden spoon (or use an electric hand whisk) until you have a smooth ball of paste.

Add the eggs gradually, beating well between each addition until the paste is smooth and glossy. Spoon the mixture into a piping bag with a 1 cm (½ inch) plain nozzle and pipe 9 cm (3½ inch) lengths of pastry diagonally on to the baking trays, leaving plenty of room between them.

Bake for 20 minutes until well risen and then reduce the temperature to 160°C/320°F/ Gas Mark 3. Cook for a further 5–10 minutes until crisp. Make a small slit in the side of each éclair to let the steam escape and return to the oven for a few minutes to dry out the centres. Cool on a wire rack.

Whip the cream and icing sugar together. When the éclairs have cooled, extend the slit and fill with the sweetened cream.

For the chocolate icing, melt the chocolate in a bowl over a pan of hot (but not boiling) water. Stir in the butter until melted and then add the icing sugar and 1–2 tablespoons of hot water to form a smooth glossy icing. Cover the top of each éclair with icing and leave to set.

Coconut slices

These traditional favourites are sweet, moist and perfect for tea parties. On a cold day, eat warm with home-made custard.

Makes 21
Preparation time:
  20 minutes + cooling
Baking time:
  25–30 minutes

110 g (4 oz) soft **margarine**
110 g (4 oz) **caster sugar**
3 **egg yolks**
225 g (8 oz) **self-raising flour**
5 tablespoons **raspberry jam**

Topping
3 **egg whites**
85 g (3 oz) **caster sugar**
140 g (5 oz) **desiccated coconut**

Preheat the oven to 180°C/350°F/Gas Mark 4. Grease a 30 x 20 cm (12 x 8 inch) Swiss roll tin.

Cream the margarine and sugar together and add the egg yolks and flour slowly to make a very stiff mixture.

Pour the mixture into the prepared tin and spread it out evenly, right to the corners. Spread with the raspberry jam.

Whisk the egg whites in a clean bowl until stiff peaks form and then add the sugar and coconut. Whisk again until the sugar has dissolved.

Spread this mixture on top of the jam and bake for 25–30 minutes until the meringue is golden. Leave to cool and then cut into slices.

Strawberry shortcakes

Old-fashioned favourites consisting of fresh strawberries and cream sandwiched between melt-in-the-mouth shortcake biscuits.

Makes 6
Preparation time:
  40 minutes + cooling
Baking time:
  8–10 minutes

225 g (8 oz) **self-raising flour**
a pinch of **salt**
25 g (1 oz) **ground almonds**
125 g (4½ oz) **butter**
60 g (2 oz) **caster sugar**, plus
  extra for sprinkling
1 **egg yolk**

To decorate
150 ml (10 fl oz) **double
  cream**
1 tablespoon **caster sugar**
250 g (9 oz) **strawberries**,
  3 reserved and the
  remainder sliced

Preheat the oven to 180°C/350°F/Gas Mark 4. Lightly grease a baking tray.

Sift the flour and salt together and mix in the ground almonds.

Cream the butter and sugar together and add the egg yolk. Work in the flour and almond mixture using your fingers to make a fine dough.

Roll the mixture out on a lightly floured surface to about 4 mm (¼ inch) thick and cut out 12 x 7 cm (2¾ inch) rounds using a fluted cutter and re-rolling as needed.

Place on the prepared tray, sprinkle with a little caster sugar and bake for 8–10 minutes. Leave to go cold.

Whip the cream, adding the sugar, and pipe a rosette on top of six of the biscuits.

Fold the sliced strawberries into the remaining cream and spoon on top of the remaining biscuits. Add the rosette-topped biscuits and decorate each with half a strawberry.

Afternoon tea biscuits

Variations of the afternoon tea biscuit feature in many of the WI recipe books of the past century. These are light and sweet with a lemony topping.

Makes 12
Preparation time:
  15 minutes
Baking time:
  15–20 minutes

80 g (3 oz) **butter**, softened
60 g (2 oz) **caster sugar**
1 **egg**, beaten
175 g (6 oz) **plain flour**
raspberry jam

Lemon icing
110 g (4 oz) **icing sugar**
lemon juice

Preheat the oven to 180°C/350°F/Gas Mark 4. Lightly grease a baking tray.

Cream the butter and sugar together and beat in three-quarters of the egg with 1 tablespoon of the flour. Add the remainder of the flour and, if necessary, the remaining egg.

Mix to a stiff paste and roll out on a lightly floured surface to about 5 mm (¼ inch) thick. Cut into 12 rounds using a 6 cm (2½ inch) cutter and re-rolling as needed.

Place on the prepared baking tray and bake for 15–20 minutes until golden brown.

While hot, coat half the biscuits with jam and sandwich the jam-coated and plain biscuits together in pairs.

To make the icing, sieve the icing sugar into a bowl and mix with lemon juice until you get the right consistency. Decorate the biscuits.

Shortbread

Traditionally associated with Scotland, classic shortbread is perfect for a vintage afternoon tea wherever you are.

Makes 10–12
Preparation time:
  15 minutes + cooling
Baking time:
  25–30 minutes

110 g (4 oz) **butter**
60 g (2 oz) **caster sugar**
140 g (5 oz) **plain flour**
80 g (3 oz) **rice flour**

Preheat the oven to 160°C/320°F/Gas Mark 3. Lightly grease two baking trays.

Cream the butter and sugar together and gradually add the flours.

Roll out on a floured surface into two 1 cm (½ inch) thick rounds. Place on the prepared baking trays.

Mark each round into triangles and bake for 25–30 minutes.

Allow to cool a little before lifting the shortbread off the baking trays on to a wire rack.

Variations For traditional variations, try one of the following.

Pitcaithly Bannock – Add 1 tablespoon of chopped peel and 1 tablespoon of chopped almonds.

Huby Bannock – Add 1 tablespoon of chopped preserved ginger and 1 tablespoon of chopped almonds.

Gingerbread

Based on a secret gingerbread recipe from the Lake District, this WI version of the classic makes a perfect gift.

Serves 12
Preparation time:
  15 minutes + cooling
Baking time:
  45 minutes

450 g (1 lb) **plain flour**
225 g (8 oz) **light brown soft sugar**, plus extra for sprinkling
2 teaspoons **ground ginger**
1 teaspoon **bicarbonate of soda**
1 teaspoon **cream of tartar**
225 g (8 oz) **margarine** or **butter**

Preheat the oven to 150°C/300°F/Gas Mark 2. Lightly grease a 30 x 25 cm (12 x 10 inch) tin.

Mix together the dry ingredients and then rub in the margarine or butter. Press the mixture into the prepared tin.

Bake for about 45 minutes. Mark into 12 bars when it comes out of the oven and sprinkle with a little extra sugar. Allow the gingerbread to cool slightly before cutting it into pieces.

Note This was first made by domestic servant Sarah Nelson in 1854. Wrap in waxed paper or non-stick baking parchment and tie with fine ribbon or string for a charming parcel.

Ginger crunchies

This name is very apt as these lightly spiced crunchy biscuits are very moreish and a perfect accompaniment to a really good cup of tea.

Makes 16
Preparation time:
  20 minutes + cooling
Baking time:
  15–20 minutes

110 g (4 oz) **butter**, softened
60 g (2 oz) **caster sugar**
140 g (5 oz) **plain flour**
1 teaspoon **baking powder**
1 teaspoon **ground ginger**
stem ginger (optional)

Topping
4 tablespoons **icing sugar**
2 tablespoons **butter**
1 teaspoon **ground ginger**
3 teaspoons **golden syrup**

Preheat the oven to 180°C/350°F/Gas Mark 4. Line a 20 cm (8 inch) square tin with foil (this makes it easier to lift the biscuits out).

Cream the butter and sugar together in a bowl. Add the flour, baking powder and ground ginger and mix well.

Press into the prepared tin and bake for 15–20 minutes.

For the topping, place all the ingredients into a small saucepan and stir over a gentle heat until mixed. Pour over the biscuit layer while still warm and cut into squares. Decorate each square with a little stem ginger, if using. Leave until cold to lift out.

Blueberry crème brûlées

We often order crème brûlée when out in a restaurant, but how many of us actually make them at home? Don't be put off – it's surprisingly easy.

Serves 4
Preparation time:
   25 minutes + 3–4 hours
   chilling + cooling
Cooking time:
   20–25 minutes

300 ml (10 fl oz) **double cream**
100 g (3½ oz) **white chocolate,**
   broken into pieces
4 **egg yolks**
25 g (1 oz) **caster sugar, plus**
   2 tablespoons **for sprinkling**
100 g (3½ oz) **fresh blueberries**

Preheat the oven to 180°C/350°F/Gas Mark 4.

Pour the cream into a saucepan and bring just to the boil. Take it off the heat, add the chocolate and leave for 5 minutes, stirring very occasionally until melted.

Whisk the egg yolks and sugar together until just mixed then gradually whisk in the warm cream mixture. Pour through a sieve back into the saucepan.

Divide the blueberries between four 150 ml (5 fl oz) ovenproof ramekin dishes and stand the dishes in a small roasting tin. Pour the custard into the dishes (the blueberries will float) then pour hot water from the tap into the roasting tin to come halfway up the sides of the dishes. Cook, uncovered, in the oven for 20–25 minutes until the desserts are just set with a slight softness to the centre.

Lift the dishes out of the tin with a cloth, leave to cool then chill in the fridge for 3–4 hours or until ready to serve.

Sprinkle the tops liberally with the remaining sugar then light a cook's torch and, holding it about 7.5 cm (3 inches) away from the sugar, gently move the torch over the top of one of the desserts until the sugar has dissolved. Continue heating until the top is golden brown then repeat with the other desserts. Leave for 5 minutes for the sugar to harden then serve within 30–40 minutes.

Tip If you don't have a cook's torch, stand the dishes in a small shallow cake tin, pack ice cubes around the dishes so that the custard stays cool, sprinkle the sugar over the top and cook under a hot grill until the sugar has dissolved and caramelised. Leave for a few minutes to harden then take the dishes out of the ice and serve.

Chocolate drop scones

Make these with Ecuadorian milk chocolate – it is the colour of dark chocolate but has a creamy, milder taste.

Serves 4
Preparation time:
 20 minutes
Cooking time: 15 minutes

175 g (6 oz) **plain flour**
1 teaspoon **baking powder**
½ teaspoons **bicarbonate of soda**
25 g (1 oz) **icing sugar**
2 **eggs**, separated
150 g (5½ oz) **low fat natural yogurt**
150 ml (5 fl oz) **semi-skimmed milk**
100 g (3½ oz) **milk chocolate (39% cocoa)**, diced
sunflower oil

Maple and chocolate sauce

8 tablespoons **maple syrup**
100 g (3½ oz) **milk chocolate (39% cocoa)**

To serve
2 ripe **peaches**, stoned and sliced, to serve
vanilla ice cream (optional)

Sift the flour, baking powder, bicarbonate of soda and icing sugar into a large bowl. In a separate bowl, whisk the egg whites until they form soft, moist-looking peaks. Add the egg yolks and yogurt to the flour mixture then gradually whisk in the milk until the mixture is thick and smooth. Fold in the diced chocolate then the egg whites.

Heat a large, non-stick frying pan or flat griddle and rub with a piece of folded kitchen towel drizzled with a little sunflower oil. Drop spoonfuls of the batter on to the pan, leaving space between each for them to rise, and cook over a medium heat until the underside is golden and the tops are bubbly. Turn over and cook the second side until golden and the centre is cooked through.

While the drop scones cook, place the maple syrup and chocolate in a small saucepan and cook over a very gentle heat, stirring occasionally until the chocolate has melted.

When the first batch of drop scones are ready, lift out of the pan and keep warm between sheets of non-stick baking paper inside a clean folded tea towel. Grease the pan again and continue until all the batter has been used up.

Arrange the drop scones on serving plates, allowing three or four per portion depending on your appetite, top with sliced peaches and drizzle with the sauce. Add a scoop of vanilla ice cream, if liked.

Tips Instead of natural yogurt and milk, try using a 284 ml carton of buttermilk. Although ordinary milk will work, the acidity in the yogurt or buttermilk works with the raising agent to make the drop scones rise that extra bit.

If you don't think you will eat all the pancakes in one sitting, then slightly undercook the ones you don't think you will have room for and reheat in a hot, greased pan later in the day.

Triple chocolate cookies

These are almost worth making just for the wonderful smell during baking. Soft, gooey and just packed with chocolate, they will be an instant hit.

Makes about 20
Preparation time:
 20 minutes + cooling
Cooking time:
 10–12 minutes

225 g (8 oz) plain flour
40 g (1½ oz) cocoa powder (no need to sift)
½ teaspoon bicarbonate of soda
150 g (5½ oz) caster sugar
100 g (3½ oz) light muscovado sugar
2 eggs, beaten
175 g (6 oz) butter, melted, plus extra for greasing
1 teaspoon vanilla essence
250 g (9 oz) mixed white, dark and milk chocolate, diced

Preheat the oven to 180°C/350°F/Gas Mark 4.

Place the flour, cocoa powder and bicarbonate of soda in a large bowl, add both sugars and fork together.

Add the eggs, melted butter and vanilla essence and roughly mix with a fork. Add the chocolate pieces and mix until well combined.

Using a small ice cream scoop or two spoons, scoop the mixture into mounds on two greased baking sheets, leaving space between them to spread during baking.

Bake for 10–12 minutes until the tops are cracked and the biscuits are a little darker but still soft. Leave to cool for a few minutes on the baking sheets to harden slightly then transfer to a wire rack to cool completely.

Tips For younger children, or adults who prefer milk chocolate, leave out the cocoa powder and add 40 g (1½ oz) of extra plain flour. Use 250 g (9 oz) of mixed milk and white diced chocolate.

For serious chocoholics, drizzle with random lines of melted white chocolate once the cookies have cooled.

Chequerboard biscuits

These eye-catching biscuits are made by alternating layers of orange and chocolate shortbread dough for a striking Battenburg cake effect.

Makes 20
Preparation time:
  30 minutes + 30 minutes
  chilling + cooling
Cooking time:
  12–15 minutes

2 tablespoons cocoa powder
4 teaspoons boiling water
225 g (8 oz) plain flour
25 g (1 oz) cornflour
175 g (6 oz) butter, cut into pieces
75 g (2¾ oz) caster sugar
grated zest of ½ an orange

Mix the cocoa powder and boiling water in a small bowl until it forms a thick paste. Set aside.

Put the flour, cornflour, butter and sugar in a bowl and rub in the butter with your fingertips or an electric mixer until the mixture looks like fine crumbs. Scoop out half the mixture (250 g/9 oz) into a separate bowl.

Add the orange zest to the first bowl, mix together then squeeze the crumbs to make a soft dough. Add the cocoa paste to the second bowl, mix together then squeeze as before to make a smooth dough.

Roll out the orange shortbread on a piece of non-stick baking paper, pressing with your fingertips to neaten the corners and make a 23 x 18 cm (9 x 7 inch) rectangle. Do the same with the chocolate shortbread on a second sheet of paper. Lift the chocolate shortbread on to the orange shortbread, peeling off the paper as you go.

Cut the stacked shortbread into three 18 cm (7 inch) long strips. Cut the first strip into four narrow 18 cm (7 inch) long strips and turn over the second and fourth strip so that the orange layer is uppermost. Push these strips together to make one strip with alternating colours in both layers.

Cut the second strip as the first one, turning the first and third narrow strips, and place these strips on top of the first four in a Battenburg pattern. You should have alternating colours in all layers. Repeat with the final strip turning the second and fourth narrow strips, to create a six-strip high biscuit that is four strips wide. Chill for 30 minutes.

Preheat the oven to 160°C/325°F/Gas Mark 3.

Cut the biscuit stack into thin slices and arrange on an ungreased baking sheet. Bake for 12–15 minutes until very lightly browned. Leave to cool on the baking sheet then transfer to a plate or biscuit tin.

Tip Rather than cut the two layered shortbread into strips, it can be rolled up and then sliced for a spiral pattern instead.

Cut 'n' come again cookies

Make up a batch of these chunky cookies and keep in the fridge. Just slice off and bake when you need them for that irresistible fresh-baked aroma.

Makes about 20
Preparation time:
  25 minutes + cooling
Cooking time: 15 minutes

250 g (9 oz) plain flour
100 g (3½ oz) light muscovado
   sugar
a pinch of salt
1 teaspoon ground cinnamon
175 g (6 oz) butter, diced, plus
   extra for greasing
75 g (2¾ oz) dark chocolate
   (70% cocoa), diced
75 g (2¾ oz) milk chocolate
   (32% cocoa), diced
50 g (1¾ oz) hazelnuts, very
   roughly chopped

Put the flour, sugar, salt and cinnamon into a bowl and mix together. Add the butter then rub in with your fingertips or an electric mixer until the mixture resembles fine crumbs. Continue mixing until the crumbs begin to stick together then squeeze with your hands until you have a rough ball.

Turn the mixture out on to a work surface (there is no need to flour first) and knead in the dark and milk chocolate and nuts.

Put on a large sheet of foil and form a 30 cm (12 inch) sausage shape with a diameter of about 5 cm (2 inches). Roll back and forth into a smooth shape. Wrap in the foil and store in the fridge until needed or for up to 3 days.

When ready to cook, preheat the oven to 180°C/350°F/ Gas Mark 4. Unwrap the biscuit dough and cut into slices about 1 cm (½ inch) thick. Transfer to greased baking sheets and bake for 15 minutes until lightly browned. Loosen the biscuits from the tray and transfer to a wire rack to cool, or serve while still slightly warm if preferred.

Tips After slicing, rewrap any remaining biscuit dough and return it to the fridge.

Experiment with flavour combinations of your own. Try 1 teaspoon of vanilla essence instead of the cinnamon, or a little finely grated orange zest. Or add some chopped dates or a little chopped glacé ginger instead of the nuts.

Raspberry choc muffins

These light, fluffy muffins are best eaten while still warm from the oven. Delicious for a special weekend brunch or for relaxing with a coffee.

Makes 12
Preparation time:
 20 minutes + cooling
Cooking time: 20 minutes

175 g (6 oz) caster sugar
125 ml (4 fl oz) sunflower oil
1 teaspoon vanilla essence
3 eggs
250 ml (9 fl oz) full fat crème
 fraîche
300 g (10½ oz) plain flour
2 teaspoons baking powder
175 g (6 oz) fresh raspberries
150 g (5½ oz) white chocolate,
 diced

Preheat the oven to 200°C/400°F/Gas Mark 6 and line a 12 hole muffin tin with paper cases or squares of non-stick baking paper.

Put the sugar, oil, vanilla essence and eggs into a large bowl and whisk together until just mixed. Add the crème fraîche and mix briefly until just smooth.

Sift in the flour and baking powder then stir together. Fold in two-thirds of the raspberries and chocolate then spoon the mixture into the paper cases. Press the remaining raspberries into the tops and sprinkle with the remaining chocolate.

Bake for about 20 minutes until the muffins are well risen, golden brown and the tops spring back when lightly pressed with a fingertip. Leave to cool for 5 minutes then lift out of the tin and transfer to a wire rack. Serve while still slightly warm.

Tip Try with blueberries or a mix of blueberries and raspberries, or use 150 g (5½ oz) of diced, ready-to-eat dried apricots instead of fresh fruit.

Gooey nut brownies

Soft, gooey, dark chocolate squares. The secret to a really good brownie is in the cooking, so keep an eye on them towards the end of the cooking time.

Cuts into 24 squares
Preparation time:
   30 minutes + cooling
Cooking time:
   20–25 minutes

250 g (9 oz) **dark chocolate**
   (70% cocoa), broken into pieces
250 g (9 oz) **butter, diced**
100 g (3½ oz) **hazelnuts**
4 **eggs**
250 g (9 oz) **caster sugar**
1 teaspoon **vanilla essence**
100 g (3½ oz) **self-raising flour**
1 teaspoon **baking powder**

Chocolate topping
75 g (2¾ oz) **dark chocolate**
   (70% cocoa), melted

Preheat the oven to 180°C/350°F/Gas Mark 4. Line a roasting tin with a base measurement of 18 x 28 cm (7 x 11 inches) with a large piece of non-stick baking paper and snip into the corners diagonally so that when the paper is pressed into the tin it lines the base and sides.

Put the chocolate and butter into a bowl and set over a saucepan of gently simmering water. Leave until melted.

Meanwhile, dry fry the hazelnuts, shaking the pan until lightly browned all over. Leave to cool then very roughly chop.

Using an electric mixer, whisk the eggs, sugar and vanilla essence together until they are very thick and a trail is left when the whisk is lifted out of the mixture. Gradually fold in the melted butter and chocolate. Sift the flour and baking powder over the top then gently fold in until just mixed. Fold in half the nuts.

Pour the mixture into the lined tin, tilt to ease the mixture into the corners then sprinkle with the remaining nuts. Bake for about 25 minutes, checking after 20 minutes, until the top is crusty and cracked and the centre is still soft and squidgy. If unsure, insert a small, fine-bladed knife into the centre – it should come out slightly smeared with chocolate. Too long in the oven and the brownies will be dry and very set. Leave to cool and harden slightly in the tin.

Lift the paper out of the tin, spoon the melted chocolate over the top of the brownies in random zigzag lines, leave to set for 15 minutes or so and then cut into 24 squares.

Tip If you are not a fan of nuts, add 100 g (3½ oz) diced white or milk chocolate or a sprinkling of ready chopped stoned dates instead.

Chocolate macaroons

These dainty, Parisian-style macaroons are crisp on the outside with a soft, slightly chewy centre.

Makes 20
Preparation time:
  30 minutes + 1 hour
  chilling + cooling
Cooking time:
  15–18 minutes

25 g (1 oz) **cocoa powder**
150 g (5½ oz) **icing sugar**
100 g (3½ oz) **ground almonds**
3 **egg whites**
a pinch **of salt**
75 g (2¾ oz) **caster sugar**
icing sugar, sifted, to decorate

Chocolate ganache filling
100 ml (3½ fl oz) **double cream**
100 g (3½ oz) **dark chocolate**
  (70% cocoa), broken into pieces

Preheat the oven to 160°C/325°F/Gas Mark 3. Line two baking sheets with non-stick baking paper and draw 2.5 cm (1 inch) circles on the underside of the paper using a tiny biscuit cutter or base of a glass as a guide.

Blend the cocoa powder, icing sugar and ground almonds together in a food processor or liquidiser then sift into a bowl.

Whisk the egg whites and salt with an electric mixer until they form stiff, moist-looking peaks then gradually whisk in the caster sugar a teaspoonful at a time until the meringue is stiff and glossy.

Gently fold in the cocoa mixture with a large serving spoon until evenly mixed then spoon into a large nylon piping bag fitted with a 1 cm (½ inch) plain piping nozzle. Pipe circles on the paper-lined baking sheets then leave at room temperature for 10 minutes.

Transfer the baking sheets to the oven and bake for 15–18 minutes until the macaroons are firm on the outside and may be easily peeled off the paper. Leave to cool on the paper.

To make the filling, bring the cream just to the boil in a small saucepan. Take off the heat, add the chocolate pieces and leave until melted. Stir until smooth then cover with cling film and chill for 1 hour or until stiff. Stir once more and use to sandwich the macaroons in pairs. Arrange on a plate and decorate with sifted icing sugar to serve.

Tips The macaroon shells can be made the day before they are needed, or even 2 days before, and kept in a biscuit tin lined with non-stick baking paper. Fill with chocolate ganache no more than 2 hours before serving or they will go very soft.

Instead of chocolate ganache, you could cheat with a little chocolate and hazelnut spread or some whipped cream flavoured with a little orange zest or peppermint essence. They also look very pretty if, once filled, they are rolled in very finely chopped pistachio nuts so that the nuts coat the filling, or if a tiny sugared viola or pansy flower is pressed on to the cream.

No-bake chocolate cake

Perhaps not a cake in the truest sense, these seriously chocolatey squares are made by melting the ingredients together rather than baking.

Cuts into 25 squares
Preparation time:
  15 minutes +
  10 minutes cooling +
  2–3 hours chilling

100 g (3½ oz) butter
100 g (3½ oz) dark chocolate
  (70% cocoa), broken into pieces
100 g (3½ oz) milk chocolate
  (32% cocoa), broken into pieces
3 tablespoons golden syrup
150 g (5½ oz) malted milk biscuits
50 g (1¾ oz) pistachios, halved
  (optional)
135 g (4¾ oz) Maltesers
100 g (3½ oz) mini pink and white
  marshmallows

Put the butter, dark and milk chocolate and golden syrup in a large mixing bowl and set it over a saucepan of gently simmering water. Leave until melted, stirring only occasionally.

Meanwhile, cut a square of non-stick baking paper a little larger than a shallow 20 cm (8 inch) cake tin, snip into the corners diagonally then press the paper into the tin so that the base and sides are lined.

Break the biscuits into rough pieces with your fingertips and stir into the chocolate mixture with the pistachios, if using. Take the bowl off the heat and allow to cool for 10 minutes or so.

Stir the Maltesers and marshmallows into the chocolate mixture then spoon into the lined tin and press into an even layer. Chill in the fridge for 2–3 hours until firm, then lift the paper from the tin, cut the cake into small squares and lift off the paper to serve.

Tip Don't be tempted to stir the Maltesers and marshmallows into the hot chocolate mix along with the biscuits or the chocolate will fall off the sweets and the marshmallows will melt and lose their shape.

Whoopies

These little cakes, sometimes known as 'pies', are the latest American craze and might even become more popular than the much loved muffin.

Makes 20
Preparation time:
  45 minutes
Cooking time:
  10–12 minutes

40 g (1½ oz) cocoa powder
4 tablespoons boiling water
250 g (9 oz) plain flour
1 teaspoon baking powder
2 teaspoons bicarbonate of soda
175 g (6 oz) light muscovado
  sugar
75 g (2¾ oz) butter, melted
150 g (5½ oz) natural yogurt
1 egg

Peanut and cream cheese
  filling

75 g (2¾ oz) salted peanuts
200 g (7 oz) cream cheese
200 g (7 oz) icing sugar, sifted

Chocolate frosting
100 g (3½ oz) dark chocolate
  (70% cocoa), broken into pieces
2–4 tablespoons milk
50 g (1¾ oz) icing sugar, sifted

Preheat the oven to 200°C/400°F/Gas Mark 6. Line three baking sheets with non-stick baking paper.

Mix the cocoa powder and boiling water together until you get a smooth paste.

Put the flour, baking powder, bicarbonate of soda and sugar into a mixing bowl and stir together. Add the cocoa paste, butter, yogurt and egg and beat together until smooth.

Pipe or spoon the mixture into fourty 5 cm (2 inch) rounds on the baking sheets, leaving space between for them to rise during baking. Leave to stand for 5 minutes.

Bake for 10–12 minutes until risen, the tops are cracked, the outside is crusty, the centre still slightly soft and the cakes can be lifted easily off the paper. Leave to cool on the paper then transfer half the cakes to a wire rack and set this over a tray.

Meanwhile, make the filling by whizzing the peanuts in a liquidiser or food processor until they are finely chopped. Beat the cream cheese and icing sugar together until just smooth then stir in the peanuts, reserving a small amount for decoration. Chill until needed.

To make the frosting, melt the chocolate with 2 tablespoons of milk in a bowl set over a saucepan of gently simmering water. Take off the heat then add the icing sugar and stir until smooth, mixing in a little extra milk if needed to make a coating consistency. Spoon the frosting over the biscuits on the wire rack then sprinkle with the reserved peanuts. Leave to set.

To finish, pipe or spoon the cream cheese filling on to the underside of the plain cakes then top with the iced cakes. Transfer to a serving plate.

Tips In true American style, these have been filled with a peanut and cream cheese filling but, for something a little more conservative, you may want to try flavouring them with a little grated orange zest and juice, some vanilla or ground cinnamon.

You could finish these dainty cakes with a homemade piped chocolate shape, piped zig zag lines of melted white or milk chocolate or bought sugar flowers.

Chocolate love hearts

A twist on chocolate éclairs, the chocolate pastry is piped into heart shapes and filled with softly whipped cream flavoured with raspberries and mint.

Makes 8
Preparation time:
  40 minutes + 15 minutes setting
Cooking time:
  13–15 minutes

50 g (1¾ oz) **butter, plus extra for greasing**
50 g (1¾ oz) **plain flour**
15 g (½ oz) **cocoa powder**
a pinch **of salt**
25 g (1 oz) **caster sugar**
2 **eggs, beaten**
½ teaspoon **vanilla essence**

To finish
250 ml (8 fl oz) **double cream**
100 g (3½ oz) **frozen raspberries, defrosted**
2 tablespoons **icing sugar**
1 tablespoon **chopped fresh mint**
75 g (2¾ oz) **dark chocolate (70% cocoa)**
15 g (½ oz) **butter**
white chocolate shavings (optional)

Put the butter and 150 ml (5 fl oz) of water in a small saucepan and bring slowly to the boil so that the butter melts. Take the pan off the heat and sift in the flour, cocoa powder and salt. Add the sugar and return the pan to the heat. Stir constantly with a wooden spoon until the mixture makes a smooth ball. Leave to cool.

Preheat the oven to 210°C/425°F/Gas Mark 7. Gradually beat the eggs and vanilla essence into the choux pastry and continue to beat until smooth.

Spoon the mixture into a nylon piping bag fitted with a 1 cm (½ inch) plain piping nozzle and pipe eight 7.5 cm (3 inch) long heart shapes on to two greased baking sheets.

Place in the oven, reduce the heat to 200°C/400°F/Gas Mark 6 and cook for 13–15 minutes until well risen and crisp.

Using a serrated knife, cut each heart in half and arrange cut sides uppermost on the baking sheets to cool.

Whip the cream until it forms soft peaks then fold in the raspberries and any juices, half the sugar and the mint and mix briefly so that the raspberries marble the cream. Spoon over the lower heart shapes then cover with the tops.

Melt the chocolate, butter and remaining icing sugar in a bowl set over a saucepan of gently simmering water, stirring occasionally until smooth. Spoon over the heart shapes and sprinkle with the white chocolate shavings, if using. Leave for 15 minutes for the frosting to harden then serve.

Tip It is always important to measure ingredients accurately, but choux pastry is one of those recipes where measurements are crucial. Not enough flour and the mixture will be too soft to pipe, too much and it will be firm and hard when cooked.

Chocolate banoffee pie

With some melted chocolate in the filling and milk chocolate digestives for the base, this favourite pudding is lifted up to a new level.

Serves 8
Preparation time:
   40 minutes + 15 minutes
   chilling + 1 hour setting

Biscuit base
75 g (2¾ oz) butter
250 g (9 oz) milk chocolate
   digestive biscuits

Banoffee topping
75 g (2¾ oz) butter
75 g (2¾ oz) dark muscovado
   sugar
400 g (14 oz) can full fat
   condensed milk
75 g (2¾ oz) dark chocolate
   (70% cocoa), broken into pieces
300 ml (10 fl oz) double cream
3 small bananas
juice of 1 lemon

To decorate
50 g (1¾ oz) dark chocolate
   (70% cocoa), melted
white chocolate curls

For the base, melt the butter in a medium saucepan. Crush the biscuits in a plastic bag using a rolling pin or in a food processor then stir into the butter until well coated. Tip into a 24 cm (9½ inch) loose-bottomed, fluted flan tin and press firmly into the base and up the sides. Chill for 15 minutes.

Wash and dry the pan then heat the butter and sugar for the topping until both have melted. Add the condensed milk and cook over a medium heat for 2–3 minutes, stirring constantly, until the mixture is just beginning to thicken and smell of toffee.

Take the pan off the heat and add the dark chocolate. Stir until melted then pour into the biscuit case. Leave to cool and set at room temperature for 1 hour.

Lift the biscuit case out of the tin and transfer to a serving plate. Whip the cream until it forms soft swirls. Slice the bananas and toss in the lemon juice. Fold two-thirds of the bananas into the cream and spoon over the toffee layer. Arrange the remaining bananas on top then drizzle with the melted dark chocolate and sprinkle with the chocolate curls. This is best served up to 3 hours after decorating.

Tip Don't want to make chocolate curls? Sprinkle with a little grated dark chocolate or a light dusting of sifted cocoa powder.

Two-tone cheesecake

A rich, American-style, baked vanilla cheesecake marbled with a dark chocolate layer and encased in a milk chocolate biscuit case.

Serves 8–10
Preparation time:
  40 minutes + cooling +
  overnight chilling
Cooking time:
  35–40 minutes

Biscuit base
75 g (2¾ oz) **butter**, plus extra for
  greasing
250 g (9 oz) **milk chocolate**
  digestive biscuits

Chocolate cheesecake
200 g (7 oz) **dark chocolate**
  (70% cocoa), broken into pieces
600 g (1 lb 5 oz) **medium-fat soft**
  cheese
100 g (3½ oz) **caster sugar**
1 teaspoon **vanilla essence**
4 **eggs**
200 ml (7 fl oz) **double cream**

Preheat the oven to 180°C/350°F/Gas Mark 4.

Melt the butter in a medium saucepan. Crush the biscuits in a plastic bag using a rolling pin or blitz in a food processor. Stir into the melted butter then tip into a buttered 23 cm (9 inch) springform tin. Press the crumbs into the base of the tin with the end of a rolling pin.

Bake for 5 minutes to set the crust then take out of the oven and reduce the temperature to 150°C/300°F/Gas Mark 2.

Meanwhile, melt the chocolate in a bowl set over a saucepan of gently simmering water. Put the cream cheese into a bowl, add the sugar and vanilla essence and mix briefly until smooth. Gradually mix in the eggs, one at a time, until smooth, then stir in the double cream and whisk for a minute or two until thick.

Ladle 300 ml (10 fl oz) of the mixture into a measuring jug. Gradually stir into the melted chocolate until smooth. Spoon half the remaining cheesecake mixture on to the biscuit case then spoon over half the chocolate mixture, filling any gaps.

Continue adding alternate teaspoonfuls of the vanilla and chocolate mixtures then, using the handle of a teaspoon, swirl the two mixtures together to give a marbled effect. Don't worry too much if the top is uneven.

Bake for 35–40 minutes or until the cheesecake is set around the edges, lightly cracked and still slightly soft in the centre. Turn the oven off, open the door and leave ajar for 1 hour. Take the cheesecake out, cool completely then transfer to the fridge overnight.

Loosen the edge of the cheesecake with a knife, remove the tin, transfer to a serving plate and cut into wedges to serve.

Tip This cheesecake can be frozen successfully as soon as it is cool. Open freeze out of the tin until firm then wrap in cling film and protect in a plastic box. Seal, label and freeze up to 6 weeks. Unwrap and defrost overnight in the fridge.

Dark chocolate mousse

Chocolate mousse is one of those wonderfully quick desserts. This one is made special by the addition of a light tangy syllabub cream.

Serves 6
Preparation time:
  25 minutes + 3–4 hours
  chilling + cooling
Cooking time: 10 minutes

200 g (7 oz) dark chocolate (70% cocoa), broken into pieces
15 g (½ oz) butter
4 tablespoons icing sugar
3 eggs, separated
finely grated zest and juice of 1 large orange
150 ml (5 fl oz) double cream
1 tablespoon brandy or orange-flavoured liqueur
sifted cocoa powder, to decorate
tuile biscuits or tiny shop bought biscuits, to serve

Put the chocolate and butter in a large bowl and set over a saucepan of gently simmering water. Leave for 10 minutes, stirring occasionally, until the chocolate has melted.

Add 2 tablespoons of icing sugar to the chocolate then gradually beat in the egg yolks, one at a time until smooth. Mix in half the orange zest and 3 tablespoons of the orange juice then take the bowl off the heat. Wrap the remaining orange zest in foil for later.

Whisk the egg whites until they form moist peaks then fold a spoonful into the chocolate mixture to loosen it slightly. Add the remaining egg whites and fold in gently until just mixed. Spoon into six small glasses or coffee cups, leave to cool then transfer to the fridge for 3–4 hours until set.

When almost ready to serve, pour the cream into a bowl, add the remaining orange zest and icing sugar and whisk until the cream softly holds its shape. Gradually whisk in 3 tablespoons of orange juice and then the brandy or liqueur. Whisk for a minute or two more until softly spoonable. Spoon on to the tops of the mousses, dust lightly with cocoa powder and serve with biscuits.

Tip When melting chocolate, check that the bottom of the bowl does not come into contact with the water and keep the heat as low as possible so that the water gently simmers and the chocolate does not overheat. If it does, you may find that the chocolate 'seizes' or sets firm the minute that the egg yolks are added, which can spoil the texture of the finished mousse.

Chocolate praline clusters

Choose three or four nuts from a mix of hazelnuts, almonds, cashews, macadamia, pecans, walnuts or pistachio nuts, or perhaps just a single nut.

Makes 12
Preparation time:
25 minutes + cooling
Cooking time:
4–5 minutes

oil, for greasing
100 g (3½ oz) granulated sugar
100 g (3½ oz) mixed blanched
   nuts, roughly chopped
1 tablespoon boiling water
15 g (½ oz) butter
100 g (3½ oz) dark chocolate
   (70% cocoa), broken into pieces

Lightly oil a 12-hole mini muffin tin and a small baking tray. Put the sugar, nuts and 5 tablespoons of cold water into a medium-sized frying pan and heat very gently, without stirring, until the sugar has dissolved.

Increase the heat and boil the syrup until it and the nuts have just turned golden. Turn the nuts very occasionally towards the end so that they brown evenly.

Take the pan off the heat and add the boiling water and butter, standing well back and tilting the pan until mixed. When the bubbles have subsided, stir lightly and spoon a little of the praline on to the oiled baking sheet. Divide the rest between the holes in the mini muffin tin and leave to cool.

Melt the chocolate in a bowl set over a saucepan of gently simmering water. Meanwhile, lift the praline off the baking sheet and finely chop.

One at a time, lift the praline clusters out of the mini muffin tin and dip into the chocolate, turning and lifting with a teaspoon and fork. Drain off the excess chocolate and put the clusters on a baking tray lined with non-stick baking paper. Repeat until all the praline clusters have been coated in the chocolate then sprinkle with the finely chopped praline. Leave to set at room temperature or in the fridge then transfer to petit four cases and arrange in a small box then tie with ribbon.

Tips Don't be tempted to stir the praline until the very end or you may crystallise the sugar syrup and spoil the texture of the caramelised sugar.

If you don't have a mini muffin tin, spoon the praline in mounds on to a lightly oiled baking sheet.

Apricot ginger florentines

Dried apricots and cranberries have been added rather than traditional glacé cherries, and the florentines have been flavoured with glacé ginger.

Makes 50
Preparation time:
  45 minutes
Cooking time:
  10–14 minutes

100 g (3½ oz) butter
100 g (3½ oz) caster sugar
1 tablespoon golden syrup
100 g (3½ oz) ready-to-eat dried
  apricots, diced
40 g (1½ oz) dried cranberries,
  chopped
2 tablespoons glacé ginger or
  drained stem ginger, chopped
50 g (1¾ oz) candied peel,
  chopped
100 g (3½ oz) flaked almonds

To decorate
100 g (3½ oz) dark chocolate
  (70% cocoa) or milk chocolate
  (32% cocoa), broken into pieces
100 g (3½ oz) white chocolate,
  broken into pieces

Preheat the oven to 180°C/350°F/Gas Mark 4. Line two baking sheets with non-stick baking paper.

Heat the butter, sugar and syrup in a saucepan until the butter has melted and the sugar dissolved. Stir in the apricots, cranberries, ginger, candied peel and almonds and mix together.

Spoon small mounds of mixture on to the baking sheets and flatten slightly. Bake for 5–7 minutes until the almonds are lightly browned. You will need to do this in batches.

Quickly neaten the edges of the florentines as they come out of the oven by putting a slightly larger plain biscuit cutter over a biscuit. Rotate the cutter to nudge the warm biscuit edges into a neat shape. Repeat with the other biscuits.

Slide the paper and florentines on to a wire rack and leave to cool and harden. Re-line the baking sheets and continue baking in batches until all the florentine mixture has been baked.

Melt the dark or milk chocolate in a bowl set over a saucepan of simmering water. Turn the florentines over, spoon the chocolate over half the biscuits and spread into an even layer. Swirl a fork through the chocolate just before it sets then chill in the fridge until firm. Cover the remainder of the florentines with melted white chocolate in the same way. Pack into a baking paper-lined box to serve.

Tip If not eating on the day of making, store the florentines in a plastic box in the fridge, interleaving the layers with non-stick baking paper.

Triple chocolate parfait

This French-style ice cream is made with a boiled sugar syrup. Serve as it is or with a little warm Maple and chocolate sauce (see page 174).

Serves 6–8
Preparation time:
40 minutes + overnight freezing

100 g (3½ oz) **dark chocolate (70% cocoa)**, broken into pieces
100 g (3½ oz) **milk chocolate (32% cocoa)**, broken into pieces
100 g (3½ oz) **white chocolate**, broken into pieces
200 g (7 oz) **caster sugar**
6 **egg yolks**
450 ml (16 fl oz) **double cream**
dark and white chocolate curls, to decorate

Melt the chocolates in three separate bowls (see Tip).

Put the sugar and 200 ml (7 fl oz) of water in a saucepan and heat gently, without stirring, until the sugar has dissolved.

Meanwhile, put the egg yolks in a large bowl. One-third fill a large saucepan with water and bring to a gentle simmer, but do not put the bowl on the pan just yet.

Increase the heat and boil the sugar syrup until it reaches 115°C (239°F) on a sugar thermometer or until a little of the syrup will make a soft ball when dropped into a glass of cold water. If the syrup forms brittle strands that snap when lifted out of the water, the syrup is too hot and it will need to be remade; if it is too soft to make a ball then it is not quite hot enough. If testing in cold water, take the pan off the heat while waiting for the syrup to cool in the water, but as a rough guide the syrup will begin to fall slowly off a spoon when it is almost ready.

As soon as the soft ball stage is reached, quickly take the pan off the heat, remove the thermometer, place the egg yolks over the simmering water then gradually whisk the hot sugar syrup into the yolks in a thin steady stream. Continue to whisk until the yolks are very thick and the mixture leaves a trail when the whisk is lifted above it.

Take the bowl off the heat and whisk for a few more minutes until the mixture is beginning to cool. Whisk the cream until it forms soft swirls then fold into the egg mixture. Divide the mixture into three equal-sized amounts then fold each into a different bowl of chocolate.

Line a 900 g (2 lb) loaf tin with a large piece of cling film then pour in the white chocolate mixture. Freeze for 15 minutes until partially set, leaving the other mixtures at room temperature.

Spoon the milk chocolate mixture over the white and spread gently into an even layer. Freeze for 15 minutes, leaving the dark chocolate mixture still at room temperature. Spoon over the final layer then freeze the parfait overnight until firm.

About 10 minutes before serving, loosen the parfait by lifting the cling film a little then cover the tin with a plate, turn the plate and tin over, lift off the tin and peel away the cling film. Decorate the top with dark and white chocolate curls and cut into thick slices with a hot knife.

Tip Rather than melting the chocolates above a saucepan of gently simmering water, you may prefer to melt them in the microwave. Use small microwaveproof bowls and set the microwave to full power. Melt the dark chocolate for 1 minute then leave to stand, then the milk chocolate for 1 minute and leave to stand. White chocolate has a tendency to burn in the microwave, so heat for 30 seconds first on medium power, check then continue in 10 second bursts until it is softened then stir. Melt the dark and milk chocolate for an extra 10 seconds each if needed, then stir.

Pear and chocolate tart

Buttery pastry encases a rich, moist filling. If you're feeling really decadent, serve with a warm brandied chocolate sauce.

Serves 6
Preparation time:
  45 minutes + 15 minutes chilling + 20 minutes cooling
Cooking time:
  45–55 minutes

Pastry
175 g (6 oz) plain flour, plus extra
  for dusting
50 g (1¾ oz) icing sugar
75 g (2¾ oz) butter, diced

Pear and chocolate filling
100 g (3½ oz) butter
100 g (3½ oz) icing sugar
100 g (3½ oz) ground almonds
a few drops of almond essence
2 eggs
100 g (3½ oz) dark chocolate
  (70% cocoa), melted
3 ripe pears (about 400 g/14 oz)
juice of ½ a lemon
2 tablespoons flaked almonds

To decorate
icing sugar
50 g (1¾ oz) dark chocolate
  (70% cocoa), diced (optional)

To make the pastry, put the flour, icing sugar and butter into a bowl and rub in the butter with your fingertips or an electric mixer until the mixture looks like fine crumbs. Add 2 tablespoons of water and mix to a smooth dough, adding a little extra water if needed.

Knead lightly then roll out on a lightly floured surface.

Butter a 24 cm (9½ inch) round, 2.5 cm (1 inch) deep, loose-bottomed fluted flan tin. Lift the pastry over a rolling pin and drape into the tin. Carefully press over the base and up the sides and trim the top to about 5 mm (¼ inch) above the top of the tin to allow for shrinkage. Prick the base and chill in the fridge for 15 minutes.

Preheat the oven to 190°C/375°F/Gas Mark 5.

Line the pastry case with greaseproof or non-stick baking paper and baking beans, put on to a baking sheet and cook for 10 minutes. Lift the paper and beans out and cook the tart for 5 more minutes until lightly browned around the edges. Reduce the oven to 180°C/350°F/Gas Mark 4.

To make the filling, beat the butter and icing sugar together until light and fluffy. Add the ground almonds, almond essence and eggs and mix until smooth. Stir in the melted chocolate.

Peel, core and quarter the pears, slice and toss in the lemon juice. Arrange just over half in the base of the tart case. Spoon the almond and chocolate mixture over the top and smooth level. Sprinkle over the remaining pears and flaked almonds.

Bake for 30–40 minutes until the mixture is set, the almonds golden and the pears on the surface are just beginning to brown. (Check after 20 minutes and cover with foil if the flaked almonds appear to be browning too quickly.) Leave to cool slightly for 20 minutes then lift out of the tin and transfer to a serving plate. Dust with icing sugar then sprinkle with extra chocolate if liked – the heat from the tart will soften it slightly. Serve cut into wedges.

Tip This tart freezes well wrapped in cling film or foil. Defrost for 3 hours at room temperature then warm through in the oven.

Summer berry fondue

Rather than serving in the traditional way, spoon summer fruits into dishes then drizzle the lusciously creamy white chocolate fondue over the top.

Serves 4
Preparation time:
  10 minutes
Cooking time:
  3–4 minutes

100 g (3½ oz) blueberries
200 g (7 oz) raspberries
200 g (7 oz) strawberries, halved
  or sliced depending on their
  size
100 g (3½ oz) white chocolate,
  broken into pieces
1 tablespoon runny honey
4 tablespoons medium white
  wine
125 ml (4½ fl oz) double cream
a few white chocolate curls, to
  decorate (optional)

Mix the fruits together then spoon into four shallow serving bowls or Champagne glasses.

Put the white chocolate, honey, wine and cream into a small saucepan and heat very gently, stirring occasionally until the chocolate has melted. You could also use a chocolate fondue set, if you have one. Spoon over the fruits and sprinkle with some chocolate curls, if liked. Serve immediately.

Tip For a dark chocolate version, simply swap the white chocolate for dark and add a little caster sugar, in place of the honey, to taste.

Chocolate banana crêpes

These thin, lacy pancakes can be rustled up in next to no time, and the chances are that you will have most of the ingredients already.

Serves 4
Preparation time:
15 minutes + 10 minutes standing
Cooking time: 15 minutes

100 g (3½ oz) plain flour
15 g (½ oz) cocoa powder
1 egg
1 egg yolk
1 tablespoon sunflower oil, plus
   extra for frying
250 ml (9 fl oz) milk

Ginger custard filling
150 ml (5 fl oz) double cream
135 g individual pot of ready
   made custard
50 g (1¾ oz) stem ginger in syrup,
   drained and chopped

To decorate
2 bananas, sliced
icing sugar, sifted
75 g (2¾ oz) dark or milk
   chocolate, melted

To make the crêpes, sift the flour and cocoa powder into a bowl, add the egg, egg yolk and 1 tablespoon of oil then gradually whisk in the milk until smooth. Leave to stand for 10 minutes.

For the filling, whip the cream until it forms soft swirls then fold in the custard and ginger.

Heat a little oil in a small frying pan, pour off the excess into a cup then add 2–3 tablespoons of the batter and tilt the pan to thinly cover. Cook for a minute or two until the underside is golden.

Loosen with a palette knife then turn or flip the crêpe and cook the second side. Slide out on to a plate and keep hot. Repeat, oiling the pan as needed until all the batter has been used up.

Fold the pancakes into quarters and arrange on plates. Spoon the custard mix in between the folds and add the banana slices. Dust lightly with icing sugar and drizzle with melted chocolate. Serve immediately.

Tip Instead of bananas and ginger, try with some fresh or frozen raspberries and passion fruit. Or, if cherries are in season, lightly cook with a little water and sugar then thicken with cornflour and spoon over the pancakes while still warm.

Chocolate French toast

There are times when you really need a sweet fix. This is great for a Sunday brunch too, maybe followed by an orange and melon salad.

Serves 2
Preparation time:
  5 minutes
Cooking time:
  5–6 minutes

40 g (1½ oz) **butter, softened**
4 **thick slices white or 50/50 white and brown bread**
50 g (1¾ oz) **milk chocolate (32% cocoa) or dark chocolate (70% cocoa), finely chopped**
1 **egg**
4 tablespoons **milk**
a few drops **of vanilla extract**
2 teaspoons **sunflower oil**
icing sugar, sifted
ground cinnamon (optional)

Spread two-thirds of the softened butter over one side of each of the slices of bread. Sprinkle two slices with the chopped chocolate then sandwich with the remaining bread, buttered side downwards, and press gently together.

Beat the egg, milk and vanilla extract in a large shallow dish, add the sandwiches and turn until evenly coated.

Heat the remaining butter and the oil in a large frying pan. Add the sandwiches, spooning any remaining egg mixture over the top, then fry until the underside is golden. Turn over and cook the second side, pressing the top gently with a fish slice so that the sandwiches stick together as the chocolate melts.

Lift out of the pan, cut into triangles or fingers and dust with sifted icing and a little cinnamon, if liked.

Chocolate cherry tiramisu

This light, fruity version is made by layering coffee-soaked biscuits with mascarpone, white chocolate and cherries from the freezer for speed.

Serves 6
Preparation time:
  15 minutes
Cooking time:
  1–1¼ minutes

225 g (8 oz) **frozen red stoned cherries**
6 tablespoons **icing sugar**
250 g (9 oz) **mascarpone cheese**
150 ml (5 fl oz) **double cream**
3 tablespoons **cherry brandy or brandy**
1 teaspoon **instant coffee**
125 ml (4½ fl oz) **boiling water**
100 g (3½ oz) **sponge finger biscuits**
75 g (2¾ oz) **white chocolate, diced**

Microwave the cherries on full power for 1–1½ minutes until defrosted then mix with 2 tablespoons of the icing sugar.

Put the mascarpone cheese and a further 2 tablespoons of icing sugar into a bowl. Gradually whisk in the cream until smooth then stir in the brandy.

Mix the coffee with the boiling water then stir in the remaining icing sugar. Dip half the biscuits into the coffee mixture, one at a time, then crumble into the bases of six glasses.

Spoon half the mascarpone mixture over the biscuits then sprinkle with half the chocolate, half the cherries and most of the cherry juice. Repeat the layers, adding the remaining white chocolate at the very end. Serve within 30 minutes.

Tip Fresh raspberries or sliced strawberries would make a delicious alternative to the cherries.

Hot raspberry trifles

Spoon down through a crisp meringue to the soft marshmallow centre then into custard, fresh raspberries and a wonderfully gooey brownie base.

Serves 4
Preparation time:
  15 minutes
Cooking time:
  12–15 minutes

175 g (6 oz) **bought or homemade chocolate brownies or chocolate sponge**
4 tablespoons **medium sherry**
175 g (6 oz) **fresh raspberries**
2 x 135 g **individual pots ready-made custard**
2 **egg whites**
75 g (2¾ oz) **caster sugar**
50 g (1¾ oz) **milk chocolate (32% cocoa), coarsely grated**

Preheat the oven to 160°C/325°F/Gas Mark 3.

Crumble the brownies or sponge into pieces and divide between four 250 ml (9 fl oz) ovenproof glass dishes. Drizzle the sherry over the top. Divide the raspberries between the dishes then spoon over the custard and level the tops.

Whisk the egg whites until they form stiff, moist-looking peaks then gradually whisk in the sugar a teaspoonful at a time until glossy. Fold in the chocolate then spoon over the dishes and swirl into peaks with the back of the spoon.

Put the dishes on a baking sheet and cook for 12–15 minutes until the peaks of the meringue are golden and the trifles are heated through.

Chestnut chocolate baskets

This easy treat is perfect to make at the last minute. It is particularly suitable for winter or Christmas entertaining.

Serves 6
Preparation time:
  15 minutes

50 g (1¾ oz) dark chocolate
   (70% cocoa), broken into pieces
150 ml (5 fl oz) double cream
250 g (9 oz) can sweetened
   chestnut spread
2 tablespoons brandy
6 brandy snap baskets
dark chocolate piped decorations

Melt the chocolate in a bowl set over a saucepan of gently simmering water.

Meanwhile, whip the cream until it forms soft swirls.

Mix the chestnut spread with the brandy until softened then stir in the melted chocolate. Fold into the cream until partially mixed for a marbled effect.

Spoon the chocolate mixture into the brandy snap baskets. Decorate with piped chocolate decorations.

Tips This creamy chocolate and chestnut mix is also delicious used to sandwich two 20 cm (8 inch) round meringues or pairs of small meringues. If you have some light muscovado sugar then use a mix of half muscovado and half caster sugar in the meringues for a light toffee flavour.

You could also decorate these baskets with dark chocolate curls and a dusting of icing sugar and cocoa powder.

Black Forest roulade

The season for fresh cherries is short, so use frozen or drained canned cherries when fresh are unavailable and decorate with chocolate curls.

Serves 8
Preparation time:
40 minutes + several
hours cooling +
marinating
Cooking time: 15 minutes

225 g (8 oz) dark chocolate
(70% cocoa), broken into pieces
5 eggs, separated
175 g (6 oz) caster sugar, plus
3 tablespoons for sprinkling
2 tablespoons hot water
250 g (9 oz) cherries on stalks
2 tablespoons kirsch
300 ml (10 fl oz) double cream
2 tablespoons icing sugar

Preheat the oven to 180°C/350°F/Gas Mark 4. Line a roasting tin with a base measurement of 34 x 23 cm (13 x 9 inches) with a large sheet of non-stick baking paper, snipping into the corners of the paper so that it lines the base and sides of the tin.

Melt 200 g (7 oz) of the chocolate in a bowl set over a saucepan of gently simmering water.

Using an electric whisk, beat the egg whites in a large bowl until they form stiff, moist-looking peaks. Using the still dirty whisk, beat the eggs yolks and sugar in a separate bowl until thick and pale and the mixture leaves a trail when the whisk is lifted above the mixture.

Fold the melted chocolate and hot water into the egg yolks until smooth. Fold in a spoonful of the egg whites to loosen the mixture then gently fold in the remaining egg whites until just mixed.

Pour into the lined tin and tilt to ease the mixture into the corners. Bake for 15 minutes until well risen and the top is crusty. Leave in the tin, cover with a clean tea towel and leave to cool for several hours.

Reserving 8 cherries on stalks for decoration, remove the stalks and stones from the remaining cherries and put into a bowl with the kirsch. Cover and leave to marinate for several hours.

About an hour before serving, pour the cream into a bowl. Add the kirsch from the cherries and the icing sugar. Whisk until the cream forms soft swirls.

Remove the tea towel from the roulade, dip in warm water, wring out and put on the work surface with a narrow edge facing you. Cover with a clean sheet of non-stick baking paper and sprinkle with the 3 tablespoons of caster sugar. Turn the roulade out on to this, remove the tin and peel off the lining paper. Mark a line about 2.5 cm (1 inch) up from the base then spoon over the cream and spread into an even layer. Sprinkle the cherries over the top and roll up the roulade, starting from the bottom edge and using the paper and tea towel to help. Transfer to a serving plate.

Melt the remaining chocolate as before and dip the reserved cherries on stalks into the chocolate until half coated. Arrange on the top of the roulade so that the melted chocolate acts as glue.

Tip This roulade can also be filled with white chocolate ganache (see chocolate flower basket, page 93, for method) using 300 ml (10 fl oz) double cream and 200 g (7 oz) white chocolate and a sprinkling of fresh raspberries and blueberries. Alternatively, spoon whipped cream over the roulade and sprinkle with a little chopped stem ginger and diced fresh mango, or fold some canned, sweetened chestnut purée into some whipped cream with a little brandy for a Christmas roulade.

Irish chocolate cake

This surprising cake is made with Guinness and cocoa powder for a moist, rich flavour that contrasts with the icing and wafer-thin chocolate curls.

Serves 10
Preparation time:
  45 minutes + cooling
Cooking time:
  50–60 minutes

150 g (5½ oz) butter, at room temperature, plus extra for greasing
50 g (1¾ oz) cocoa powder, plus 1 tablespoon for dusting
175 g (6 oz) plain flour
1 teaspoon bicarbonate of soda
½ teaspoon baking powder
250 g (9 oz) caster sugar
3 eggs, beaten
200 ml (7 fl oz) Guinness

Frosting
2 egg whites
100 g (3½ oz) icing sugar
175 g (6 oz) butter, diced, at room temperature
¼ teaspoon vanilla essence
200 g (7 oz) white chocolate curls

Preheat the oven to 160°C/325°F/Gas Mark 3. Butter and dust a 20 cm (8 inch) springform tin with the 1 tablespoon of cocoa powder.

Sift the cocoa powder, flour, bicarbonate of soda and baking powder together into a medium bowl. In a second, larger bowl, cream the remaining butter and sugar together until light and fluffy. Alternately mix in spoonfuls of egg and the flour mixture until all the eggs and flour have been added.

Gradually mix in the Guinness until smooth then pour the cake mixture into the lined tin. Smooth the surface and bake for 50–60 minutes until well risen, the top has slightly cracked and a skewer comes out clean when inserted into the centre of the cake.

Leave to cool in the tin for 10 minutes then loosen the edge, turn out on to a wire rack and peel off the lining paper.

Using a hand-held electric whisk, and in a bowl set over a saucepan of simmering water, whisk the egg whites and icing sugar for about 5 minutes until very thick and glossy. Take the bowl off the heat and whisk for a few more minutes until cool. Gradually whisk in the butter, little by little (don't try to hurry this stage), until all the butter has been added and the frosting is smooth and glossy. Mix in the vanilla essence. If the frosting is too soft to spread, chill for 30 minutes.

Cut the cake into three layers horizontally then sandwich back together with half of the frosting. Spoon a thin layer of frosting over the top and sides of the cake to stick the crumbs in place, then spread the remainder over the cake. Transfer to a serving plate and decorate with the chocolate curls. Store in a cool place until ready to serve.

Tip If the icing begins to split when you add the butter, add 1 tablespoon of hot water and whisk well before adding any extra butter.

Chocolate thins

These must be the easiest petits fours to make. They look particularly attractive if different batches are made with white, milk and dark chocolate.

Makes 30
Preparation time:
10 minutes + 1 hour chilling

100 g (3½ oz) **dark chocolate (70% cocoa)**, broken into pieces
1 tablespoon **runny honey**
grated zest of ½ a small **orange** and 1 tablespoon **orange juice**
grated zest of ½ a **lime** and 2 teaspoons **lime juice**
75 g (2¾ oz) **fruit and nut selection**, roughly chopped (see Tip)
1 tablespoon **pumpkin seeds**, roughly chopped

Melt the chocolate and honey in a bowl set over a saucepan of gently simmering water. Stir in the orange and lime zest and juice until smooth and glossy.

Drop well-spaced, heaped teaspoonfuls of the mixture on to a baking sheet lined with non-stick baking paper. Spread each into a round about 4 cm (1½ inches) wide with the back of the spoon.

Sprinkle with the chopped fruit and nut mixture and pumpkin seeds then chill in the fridge until firm. Peel off the paper and pack into a small box lined with a clean square of non-stick baking paper. Add a lid and tie with ribbon.

Tip Fruit and nut selection is a gourmet-style blend that often includes whole cashews, unblanched almonds, pecans, pistachio nuts, dried cranberries, raisins and sultanas. It is sold in packs alongside the other nuts and seeds in the supermarket and is a cheap way of using a wide selection of fruit and nuts in a small quantity. You could also use a breakfast cereal topper or make up your own mix, depending on what you have in your cupboard.

Peppermint creams

These are fun to make with young children. Choose different shaped cutters, making sure that they are bite-sized, and have fun with the colours.

Makes 80
Preparation time:
   25 minutes + 2–3 hours drying

1 tablespoon liquid glucose
1 egg white or dried egg white powder reconstituted with water
a few drops of peppermint essence
500 g (1 lb 2 oz) icing sugar, sifted, plus extra for dusting
pink and mauve edible paste colouring
100 g (3½ oz) dark chocolate (70% cocoa), broken into pieces

Put the liquid glucose, egg white and a little peppermint essence into a bowl or food processor and gradually mix in enough icing sugar to make a ball. If not using a processor, start with a wooden spoon and then squeeze the mixture with your hands when it becomes too stiff to mix. You may not need all the sugar.

Knead until smooth on a work surface dusted with a little icing sugar. Cut the dough in half. Knead a little pink colouring into one half and a little mauve into the other half so that the food colourings make a marbled effect.

Roll out the pink icing thinly then cut out heart shapes or circles with tiny biscuit cutters. Reroll the trimmings and continue until it is all used up. Repeat with the mauve icing.

Leave the peppermint creams to dry on baking sheets lined with non-stick baking paper for at least 2 hours.

Melt the dark chocolate in a bowl set over gently simmering water. Dip the peppermint creams, one at a time, into the chocolate until they are half covered then leave to dry on the paper-lined trays. Pack into small boxes to serve.

Lavender chocolate cake

Made with thick-set lavender honey and lavender flowers, this cake makes a great talking point. For a birthday, add some fine candles and a ribbon.

Serves 8–10
Preparation time:
30 minutes + 30 minutes firming + cooling
Cooking time:
40–45 minutes

oil for greasing
50 g (1¾ oz) **cocoa powder, plus 1 tablespoon for dusting**
175 g (6 oz) **plain flour**
1½ teaspoons **bicarbonate of soda**
1½ teaspoons **baking powder**
1 teaspoon **dried or 2 teaspoons fresh lavender petals, plus extra to decorate**
50 g (1¾ oz) **caster sugar**
150 ml (5 fl oz) **virgin olive oil**
150 ml (5 fl oz) **milk**
3 **eggs**
100 g (3½ oz) **runny lavender honey**
lavender flowers on their stems, to decorate
whipped cream, to serve

Frosting

100 g (3½ oz) **thick-set lavender honey**
200 g (7 oz) **dark chocolate (70% cocoa), broken into pieces**
50 g (1 oz) **icing sugar**
1 tablespoon **hot water**

Preheat the oven to 160°C/325°F/Gas Mark 3. Lightly oil a 20 cm (8 inch) springform tin, sprinkle over 1 tablespoon of cocoa powder and tilt the tin until the base and sides are well coated.

Sift the remaining cocoa powder, flour, bicarbonate of soda and baking powder into a large bowl then stir in the lavender petals and sugar. Mix the oil, milk and eggs together in a jug.

Add the honey to the flour then gradually whisk in the oil mixture until smooth.

Pour the cake mixture into the tin and level the surface. Bake for 40–45 minutes until well risen and a skewer comes out clean when inserted into the centre of the cake. Leave to cool for 10 minutes, loosen the edge and turn out of the tin on to a wire rack. Leave to cool.

To make the frosting, warm the honey and chocolate in a bowl over a saucepan of barely simmering water, stirring occasionally until the chocolate has melted. Sift the icing sugar and stir into the chocolate with the hot water until the frosting is smooth.

Leave the cake on the wire rack, slide a plate underneath to catch any frosting drips and spoon the frosting over the top and sides of the cake. Smooth with a round bladed knife and swirl the top attractively. Sprinkle the top of the cake with a few extra lavender petals and some flowers still on their stems. Leave for 30 minutes for the frosting to firm up then transfer to a serving plate. Serve cut into slices with whipped cream sprinkled with lavender petals.

Tips Not a fan of lavender? Leave it out and use mixed flower or clover honey, adding a little grated orange zest instead.

If you like, you could cut the cake in half horizontally and use a few spoonfuls of the frosting to sandwich it back together again.

Three-tiered chocolate cake

Spoil milk chocolate fans with this light chocolate cake decorated with pink fondant icing flowers – easily made with plunger cutters.

Serves 40
Preparation time:
  2 hours + cooling +
  setting
Cooking time:
  20–35 minutes

500 g (1 lb 2 oz) **butter, at room temperature**
500 g (1 lb 2 oz) **caster sugar**
9 **eggs**
625 g (1 lb 6 oz) **self-raising flour**
75 g (2¾ oz) **cocoa powder**
4–6 tablespoons **milk**

Fondant flowers
350 g (12 oz) **ready-to-roll white icing**
brown and pink or red paste food colourings
cornflour, for dusting

Butter icing
250 g (9 oz) **dark chocolate, broken into pieces**
250 g (9 oz) **butter, at room temperature**
500 g (1 lb 2 oz) **icing sugar, sifted**
2 tablespoons **milk**

Preheat the oven to 160°C/325°F/Gas Mark 3. Line the bases and sides of a 20 cm (8 inch), a 15 cm (6 inch) and a 7.5 cm (3 inch) deep, round cake tin with non-stick baking paper (see Tip).

Cream the butter and sugar together until smooth. Add the eggs one at a time, alternating with a little flour and mixing in each until smooth.

Add the remaining flour, cocoa powder and enough milk to make a soft dropping consistency. Divide the mixture between the cake tins so they are all a similar height. Smooth the tops.

Bake all the cakes on the centre shelf, allowing about 40–45 minutes for the small cake, about 1 hour for the middle cake and 1 hour 20–35 minutes for the largest one or until a skewer inserted into the centre comes out clean. Leave to cool for 10 minutes then turn out on to a wire rack, peel off the paper and cool completely.

Meanwhile, make the flowers. Divide the icing into four and colour one piece brown and the others varying shades of pink. Wrap each piece of icing separately in cling film so it does not dry out.

Taking a little icing at a time, roll out thinly on a work surface dusted with cornflour. Stamp out flowers with plunger cutters then press into a circle of foam so that the petals curl. Transfer to a tray lined with non-stick baking paper and continue – rolling and stamping until you have a large selection of different sized flowers. Leave to dry and harden for at least 1 hour.

To make the butter icing, melt the chocolate in a bowl set over a saucepan of simmering water. Beat the butter with the sugar until light and fluffy then gradually mix in the chocolate until smooth. Stir in the milk, if needed, to make a soft, spreadable icing.

Trim the cakes so the tops are level then cut each into three layers. Sandwich back together with some of the butter icing.

Put the largest cake on a plate and stack the smaller cakes on top, sticking them in place with a little butter icing and securing them with 2 or 3 long wooden skewers. Spread a little of the butter icing thinly over the tops and sides of the cakes to stick the crumbs in place, then spread most of the remaining icing over more thickly and smooth with a palette knife. Keep a little icing aside for the flowers.

Arrange the flowers over the cake in swathes, right down to the plate, sticking some of the smallest flowers inside the largest ones with tiny dots of butter icing. Leave in a cool place for up to 24 hours or until ready to serve.

Tip To bake the top tier, wash and dry an empty 200 g (7 oz) baked bean or similar can. Remove the top completely then line with non-stick baking paper and put on a baking sheet with the middle sized cake tin.

Strawberry layer cake

This light, whisked sponge is the ideal cake for those that find dark chocolate a little too rich and bitter for their taste.

Serves 8
Preparation time:
 40 minutes + cooling
Cooking time: 10 minutes

4 eggs
100 g (3½ oz) caster sugar
100 g (3½ oz) plain flour
15 g (½ oz) cocoa powder

To decorate
300 ml (10 fl oz) double cream
grated zest of 1 lime
2 tablespoons icing sugar
4 tablespoons chocolate and
 hazelnut spread
400 g (14 oz) small strawberries,
 sliced
100 g (3½ oz) milk chocolate
 (32% cocoa), coarsely grated

Preheat the oven to 200°C/400°F/Gas Mark 4. Line a 33 x 23 cm (13 x 9 inch) Swiss roll tin with a slightly larger piece of non-stick baking paper and snip diagonally into the corners so that the paper lines the base and stands a little above the sides of the tin.

Put the eggs and sugar in a large bowl and whisk with an electric mixer until very thick, pale and mousse-like and the mixture leaves a trail when the whisk is lifted slightly above the mixture.

Sift the flour and cocoa powder over the top then, using a large spoon, gently fold into the whisked eggs in a figure of eight movement. Pour into the prepared tin and tilt the tin to ease the mixture into the corners. Do not spread the mixture or you will knock out the air.

Bake for 10 minutes or until the sponge is well risen and beginning to shrink away from the sides of the tin and the centre springs back when lightly pressed with a fingertip. Leave to cool in the tin.

Lift the sponge and lining paper out of the tin and put on to a chopping board. Trim the outer edge off the two short sides, cut the sponge into three 23 cm (9 inch) long strips and loosen from the paper.

Pour the cream into a bowl, add the lime zest and icing sugar and whisk until it forms soft swirls. Lift one of the sponge strips off the paper and put towards the end of the chopping board. Spread with 2 tablespoons of the chocolate spread then a little of the cream and a thin layer of sliced strawberries, keeping the smaller slices for the very top.

Cover with a second sponge strip and repeat. Add the third sponge strip and press down lightly. Spread the remaining cream thinly over the top and sides of the cake and arrange the remaining strawberry slices in rows over the top. Press the grated chocolate over the sides of the cake with a wide-bladed knife, carefully transfer to a serving plate and keep in the fridge until ready to serve.

Tips If you don't have a Swiss roll tin, measure across the base of the roasting tins that you have and you may find that one of these will be the right size.

If you don't have an electric whisk, put the mixing bowl over a saucepan of gently simmering water and beat with a balloon whisk. The hot water will help to speed up the whisking time but you will still need plenty of elbow grease!

Devil's food cake

A retro favourite made by mixing cocoa to a smooth paste before adding it to the mixture. The cake is filled and coated with a glossy butter icing.

Serves 6
Preparation time:
40 minutes + cooling
Cooking time:
50–60 minutes

50 g (1¾ oz) cocoa powder
200 ml (7 fl oz) boiling water
175 g (6 oz) plain flour
¼ teaspoon baking powder
1 teaspoon bicarbonate of soda
100 g (3½ oz) white vegetable
    shortening or butter
250 g (9 oz) caster sugar
2 eggs

Frosting
150 g (5½ oz) dark chocolate
    (70% cocoa), broken into pieces
200 g (7 oz) butter, at room
    temperature
200 g (7 oz) icing sugar
milk and white chocolate curls, to
    decorate

Preheat the oven to 160°C/325°F/Gas Mark 3. Line the base and sides of an 18 cm (7 inch) deep, round cake tin with non-stick baking paper.

Put the cocoa powder in a bowl and gradually mix in the boiling water until smooth. Leave to cool.

Mix the flour with the baking powder and bicarbonate of soda in a small bowl. Cream the shortening or butter with the sugar. Beat in one of the eggs then add a spoonful of the flour and beat until smooth. Add the second egg and gradually beat in the remaining flour then the cocoa paste, mixing well until smooth.

Pour into the lined tin, level the surface and bake for 50–60 minutes until well risen and a skewer comes out clean from the centre. Leave to cool for 10 minutes then transfer to a wire rack and peel away the lining paper.

To make the frosting, melt the chocolate in a bowl set over a saucepan of gently simmering water. Beat the butter and sugar together in a second bowl until smooth then gradually beat in the chocolate until smooth and glossy.

Cut the cake into three layers then sandwich back together with some of the frosting. Spread the remainder over the top and sides of the cake and swirl with a round-bladed knife. Transfer to a flat plate and decorate the top with chocolate curls.

Tip If the frosting is very soft when first spread over the cake, transfer to the fridge for 30 minutes or so to firm up.

Chocolate amaretti torte

Surprisingly, this striking, two-tone sponge casing is not as tricky to create as you may think. The secret is not to overcook the sponge.

Serves 10
Preparation time:
 45 minutes + chilling
Cooking time:
 5–6 minutes

4 eggs, separated
90 g (3¼ oz) caster sugar
2 egg yolks
15 g (½ oz) plain flour
40 g (1½ oz) cornflour
15 g (½ oz) cocoa powder
5 strawberries, halved
cocoa powder, sifted, to decorate
 (optional)

Filling
200 g (7 oz) dark chocolate
 (70% cocoa), broken into pieces
300 g (10½ oz) ready made
 custard
3 tablespoons amaretto liqueur
 or brandy
450 ml (16 fl oz) double cream
75 g (2¾ oz) amaretti biscuits,
 crushed

Preheat the oven to 200°C/400°F/Gas Mark 6. Line three baking sheets with non-stick baking paper, drawing two 20 cm (8 inch) circles on two of the pieces of paper and a 33 x 15 cm (13 x 6 inch) rectangle on the third.

Using an electric mixer, whisk the egg whites until they form stiff, moist-looking peaks then gradually whisk in one-third of the sugar. Using the still dirty whisk, beat all the egg yolks and remaining sugar until thick and mousse-like and the mixture leaves a trail when the whisk is lifted up. Fold in the egg whites, then spoon half the mixture back into the egg white bowl.

Sift the flour and half the cornflour into one of the bowls and gently fold in. Sift the cocoa powder and remaining cornflour over the second bowl and fold in.

Spoon the plain mixture into a large piping bag fitted with a 8 mm (³/₈ inch) plain piping nozzle. Pipe diagonal lines over all the drawn shapes, leaving a nozzle width between each line. Pipe the chocolate mixture into the gaps then bake for 5–6 minutes until the sponge is just cooked and beginning to colour. You may need to cook in two batches.

Quickly invert the rectangle of sponge on to a fresh piece of non-stick baking paper, peel off the lining paper, trim to the size of the original drawn rectangle then cut into two long thin strips. Press the sponge strips around the inside of a 20 cm (8 inch) springform tin, with the lightest side touching the tin.

Trim the sponge circles to a little smaller than the base of the springform tin. Keep the best one for the top and press the other into the base of the tin.

Melt the chocolate in a bowl set over a saucepan of gently simmering water. Take the bowl off the pan and stir in the custard then the liqueur or brandy. Whip the cream until only just beginning to thicken then gradually whisk in the chocolate custard. Stir in the amaretti biscuits then pour into the sponge-lined tin. Add the remaining sponge circle, paler side upwards and press gently down on to the filling.

Chill for 5 hours or overnight, remove from the tin and cut into wedges. Serve with the strawberries. Dust the plate lightly with sifted cocoa, if liked.

Tips This also tastes delicious served with a drizzle of warm dark chocolate sauce.

This dessert can also be frozen (pack into a plastic container for protection). Defrost in the fridge.

Beetroot chocolate cake

This might sound like a strange combination but it works incredibly well. The beetroot adds a moistness and depth to the cake that everyone loves.

Serves 10
Preparation time:
 45 minutes + cooling
Cooking time:
 1–1¼ hours

250 g (9 oz) **chilled vacuum pack of cooked beetroot in natural juices, drained**
250 g (9 oz) **butter, at room temperature**
250 g (9 oz) **caster sugar**
4 **eggs**
250 g (9 oz) **self-raising flour**
50 g (2 oz) **cocoa powder**
1 teaspoon **vanilla essence**

Butter icing
125 g (4½ oz) **butter, at room temperature**
250 g (9 oz) **icing sugar**
½ teaspoon **vanilla essence**
1 tablespoon **milk**

To decorate
mauve paste food colouring
500 g (1lb 2 oz) **ready-to-roll fondant icing**
cornflour, for dusting
50 g (1¾ oz) **dark chocolate (70% cocoa), melted**
1 m (40 inches) x 2.5 cm (1 inch) **wide brown ribbon**

Preheat the oven to 160°C/325°F/Gas Mark 3. Line the base and sides of a 20 cm (8 inch) deep, round, loose-bottomed cake tin with non-stick baking paper.

Purée the beetroot in a food processor until smooth then scoop out and reserve. Add the butter and sugar to the processor and cream together until light and fluffy.

Gradually mix in the eggs, one at a time, adding a little of the flour after each addition and mixing until smooth before adding the next egg.

Add the remaining flour, cocoa powder and vanilla essence. Mix until smooth then beat in the beetroot purée.

Spoon the mixture into the tin, level the surface and bake for 1–1¼ hours or until well risen, the top is slightly cracked and a skewer comes out clean when inserted into the centre of the cake. (You may need to cover the top of the cake after 45 minutes or so if seems to be browning too quickly.) Leave to cool in the tin for 10 minutes then transfer to a wire rack to cool completely.

To make the icing, beat the butter, half the icing sugar, vanilla essence and milk together until smooth then gradually beat in the remaining sugar. Peel the paper off the cake, cut horizontally into three thin layers then sandwich back together with half the butter icing. Spread the remaining icing thinly over the top and sides of the cake. Transfer to a serving plate.

Knead a little food colouring into the ready-to-roll icing and roll out on a surface lightly dusted with cornflour until you have a circle of about 30 cm (12 inches) in diameter. Lift over the rolling pin, drape over the cake and smooth in place with hands dusted in cornflour. Trim off excess icing and brush away any remaining cornflour from the cake.

Spoon the melted chocolate into a greaseproof paper piping bag, fold the top down securely and snip a tiny amount from the tip with scissors. Mark a circle in the centre of the cake with a 7.5 cm (3 inch) plain biscuit cutter and pipe dots of chocolate on the marked circle (don't pipe them too close together or they will merge together). Pipe swirls and dots of chocolate over the top of the cake. Leave in a cool place for the decoration to set then finish with a ribbon around the sides of the cake. Secure in place with dot of melted chocolate or a pin, but remember to remove the pin just before serving the cake.

Tips If you don't have a food processor, mash the beetroot or roughly chop and purée in small batches in a liquidiser.

For a special occasion, place fine candles just inside the circle in the centre of the cake.

This is also delicious and moist served plain without the buttercream or fondant icing; whipped cream makes a good accompaniment.

Christmas cake

Unusually, this rich fruit cake is flavoured with melted chocolate and glacé ginger for a festive cake with a twist.

Serves 20
Preparation time: 40 minutes + 3 hours soaking or overnight + 1 week feeding + cooling
Cooking time: 2¾–3¼ hours

4 tablespoons brandy, plus 8 tablespoons to finish
grated zest and juice of 1 lemon
grated zest and juice of 1 orange
2 x 500 g (1 lb 2 oz) bags luxury dried fruit
300 g (10½ oz) plain flour
2 tablespoons cocoa powder
1 teaspoon ground cinnamon
1 teaspoon ground allspice
250 g (9 oz) butter, at room temperature
250 g (9 oz) light muscovado sugar
5 eggs, beaten
2 tablespoons chopped glacé ginger
50 g (1¾ oz) pistachio nuts, left whole
100 g (3½ oz) dark chocolate (70% cocoa), broken into pieces and melted

Put the 4 tablespoons of brandy and lemon and orange zest and juices into a medium saucepan and bring just to the boil. Add the dried fruit and stir together. Cover and leave to soak for 3 hours or overnight, stirring very occasionally.

Preheat the oven to 140°C/275°F/Gas Mark 1. Line the base and sides of a deep 23 cm (9 inch) round cake tin with a double thickness of non-stick baking paper and set aside.

Mix the flour, cocoa powder and spices together. Using an electric mixer, cream the butter and sugar together in a large bowl until light and fluffy then gradually add alternate spoonfuls of beaten egg and flour, mixing between each addition until smooth.

When the eggs and flour mix have all been added, gradually mix in the soaked fruit then the ginger and pistachio nuts. Gradually mix in the melted chocolate.

Spoon the cake mixture into the prepared tin and level the surface. Bake for 2¾–3¼ hours or until a skewer comes out clean when inserted into the centre of the cake.

Leave the cake to cool in the tin then take out and wrap in foil. Feed the cake with 2 tablespoons of brandy every other day for a week. Leave to mature for 3–4 weeks, if time. Decorate as desired.

Chocolate mousse cake

This is an incredibly rich, dark chocolate cake that is ideal for those with a gluten intolerance, but do check that the chocolate is also gluten free.

Serves 8
Preparation time:
  30 minutes + cooling
Cooking time:
  25–30 minutes

250 g (9 oz) dark chocolate
  (70% cocoa), broken into pieces
100 g (3½ oz) butter, diced, plus
  extra for greasing
6 cardamom pods
1 tablespoon cocoa powder, plus
  extra for decorating
5 eggs, separated
150 g (5½ oz) caster sugar
2 teaspoons warm water
crème fraîche, to serve

Apricot compote
200 g (7 oz) ready-to-eat dried
  apricots, sliced
4 cardamom pods, roughly
  crushed
2 tablespoons honey
juice of 1 lemon
250 ml (9 fl oz) water

Put the chocolate and butter in a bowl. Crush the cardamom pods with a pestle and mortar, discard the green pods and finely grind the black seeds. Add these to the chocolate and melt over a saucepan of gently simmering water.

Preheat the oven to 180°C/350°F/Gas Mark 4. Butter a 23 cm (9 inch) springform tin, add the cocoa powder and tilt the tin until the base and sides are completely covered. Discard the excess.

Using an electric mixer, whisk the egg whites in a large bowl until they form stiff peaks then gradually whisk in half the sugar, a teaspoonful at a time. Whisk for a minute or two more until thick and glossy. Using the still dirty whisk, whisk the egg yolks and remaining sugar in a second large bowl until thick and pale.

Gradually whisk the melted chocolate and butter mixture into the egg yolks. Fold in the warm water then a large spoonful of the egg whites to loosen the mixture. Gently fold in the remaining egg whites and spoon the mixture into the prepared tin.

Bake for 25–30 minutes until the cake is well risen, the top is crusty and has cracked and the centre is still slightly soft. Leave to cool in the tin – the cake will sink and crack more on cooling.

Meanwhile put all the compote ingredients into a saucepan, cover and heat gently for 5 minutes until softened. Set aside.

When ready to serve, loosen the edge of the cake, remove from the tin and transfer to a serving plate. Cut into wedges, dust lightly with sifted cocoa powder and serve with spoonfuls of crème fraîche and the apricot compote.

Tip Don't have a pestle and mortar? Improvise with the end of a rolling pin and a mug.

Chocolate truffle cake

Finding the perfect cake for the man in your life can be tricky. This mix of extra-dark chocolate cake and boozy truffles could be the answer.

Serves 24
Preparation time:
1½ hours + cooling
Cooking time: 1–1¼ hours

150 g (5 oz) **cocoa powder**
400 ml (14 fl oz) **boiling water**
250 g (9 oz) **butter**
500 g (1 lb 2 oz) **light muscovado sugar**
5 **eggs**
400 g (14 oz) **plain flour**
2 teaspoons **baking powder**

Butter icing

20 g (¾ oz) **cocoa powder**
2 tablespoons **boiling water**
150 g (5½ oz) **butter, at room temperature**
300 g (10½ oz) **icing sugar**
2 tablespoons **rum or brandy (to match flavouring in truffles)**

To decorate

200 g (7 oz) **white chocolate melted**
300 g (11 oz) **dark chocolate melted**
26 **small** and 16 **large Brandy truffles (see page 232)**

Preheat the oven to 180°C/350°F/Gas Mark 4. Line the base and sides of an 18 cm (7 inch) and a 12 cm (5 inch) deep, square cake tin with non-stick baking paper.

Put the cocoa powder into a bowl and gradually whisk in the boiling water until smooth. Leave to cool.

Cream the butter and sugar together until smooth. Beat the eggs in one at a time, adding a little flour after each egg and beating well until smooth. Gradually mix in the remaining flour, baking powder and cocoa paste and beat well until smooth.

Divide between the cake tins so that both are a similar depth and smooth the tops. Bake for about 45–55 minutes for the small cake and 1–1¼ hours for the larger one or until well risen, the top is crusty and firm but the centre still very slightly soft (test with a skewer). Leave to cool in the tins.

To make the butter icing, mix the cocoa powder with the boiling water until you get a smooth paste then leave to cool. Beat the butter and sugar together until smooth then mix in the cocoa paste and rum or brandy.

Turn the cakes out of the tins, peel off the lining paper and trim the tops level if necessary. Cut each cake into three layers then sandwich back together with some of the butter icing. Spread a little butter icing on top of the larger cake, press the smaller cake on top and secure in place with long wooden skewers. Put on a flat plate or cake board. Spread the remaining butter icing over the tops and sides of the cakes.

Cut four pieces of non-stick baking paper or clear acetate the same size as the sides of the larger cake, and four pieces the same as the sides of the smaller cake. Pipe the white chocolate over the paper or acetate in random squiggles and chill on a baking sheet in the fridge until hard. Spread half the dark chocolate over two small and two large pieces of paper or acetate to create a marbled effect. Press one of the small pieces on to one of the sides of the top cake so that the chocolate is touching the butter icing. Press in place then repeat on the opposite side. Do the same to the lower cake, chill until firm then carefully peel away the paper or acetate. Re-melt the remaining dark chocolate and repeat so that all the sides of the cakes are covered, trimming away any excess paper or acetate so that the sides meet but do not overlap.

Arrange the smaller truffles around the base of the small cake and the larger ones in rows on the very top.

Tips Spread a little dark chocolate on to a piece of non-stick baking paper or acetate, cut into a small rectangle leave to set, then pipe on a name, as if it's a gift card. Chill then peel away the paper and tuck the chocolate among the truffles.

Clear acetate is available from good stationery shops. If you cannot find it, use non-stick baking paper instead.

Coconut meringue cake

This coconut-speckled, macaroon-style meringue is flecked with grated chocolate and finished with cream and pineapple tossed with lime zest.

Serves 8
Preparation time:
  30 minutes + 10 minutes
  standing + cooling
Cooking time:
  25–30 minutes

5 egg whites
¼ teaspoon cream of tartar
225 g (8 oz) caster sugar
1 teaspoon white wine vinegar
75 g (2¾ oz) dark chocolate
  (70% cocoa), coarsely grated
75 g (2¾ oz) unsweetened
  desiccated coconut

To finish
4 slices fresh pineapple, peeled,
  cored and diced
finely grated zest of 1 lime
250 ml (9 fl oz) double cream
coconut curls (optional, see Tip)
25 g (1 oz) dark chocolate
  (70% cocoa), melted

Preheat the oven to 160°C/325°F/Gas Mark 3. Lightly oil two 20 cm (8 inch) sandwich tins and line the bases with a circle of greaseproof or non-stick baking paper.

Whisk the egg whites and cream of tartar together until they form stiff, moist-looking peaks. Gradually whisk in the sugar, a teaspoonful at a time, and continue whisking for a minute or two until the meringue is thick and glossy. Mix in the vinegar.

Fold in the grated chocolate and coconut with a large spoon and divide the meringue between the two prepared tins. Spread evenly then swirl the tops with the back of the spoon.

Bake for 25–30 minutes until the top of the meringue is crisp and very pale golden. Loosen the edges with a round-bladed knife, leave for a couple of minutes then turn out on to a wire rack (the meringues are very fragile, so turn out carefully). Leave to cool.

When almost ready to serve, mix the pineapple and lime zest together. Whip the cream until it forms soft swirls. Peel the lining paper from the meringues then transfer one to a serving plate.

Spoon on just over half the cream and spread to the edges of the cake then add just over half the pineapple. Add the second meringue and decorate with the remaining cream, pineapple and coconut curls, if using. Drizzle with the melted chocolate in random zigzag lines. Leave to stand for 10 minutes then serve.

Tips To make coconut curls, pierce one of the three eyes in the top of the coconut with a skewer or small knife. One of the eyes will be easy, the other two impossible. Tip out the milk into a glass then break the coconut into large pieces by hitting on a very hard surface. Prise the white coconut flesh from the outer shell then pare into thin ribbons with a swivel-bladed vegetable peeler.

For a true taste of the Caribbean, you might like to add a little rum to the whipped cream.

Birthday cake squares

You are never too old to enjoy chocolate birthday cake topped with a rich chocolate and cream cheese frosting and chocolate buttons.

Makes 24 squares
Preparation time:
  30 minutes + firming + cooling
Cooking time: 30 minutes

225 g (8 oz) **soft margarine**
225 g (8 oz) **caster sugar**
175 g (6 oz) **self-raising flour**
50 g (1¾ oz) **cocoa powder**
1½ teaspoons **baking powder**
4 **eggs**

Toppings
100 g (3½ oz) **milk chocolate,** **broken into pieces**
200 g (7 oz) **cream cheese**
300 g (10½ oz) **icing sugar, sifted**
24 **small birthday candles and** **candle holders**
a selection of **white and dark** **chocolate buttons, sweets and** **sugar sprinkles**

Preheat the oven to 180°C/350°F/Gas Mark 4. Line a roasting tin with a base measurement of 18 x 28 cm (7 x 11 inches) with a large piece of non-stick baking paper, snipping into the corners of the paper and pressing it into the roasting tin so that the base and sides are lined.

Put all the cake ingredients into a bowl and beat until smooth (or use a food processor). Spoon the mixture into the tin and level the surface.

Bake for about 30 minutes until well risen and the cake springs back when pressed in the centre with a fingertip. Leave to cool in the tin for 10 minutes then lift the paper and cake out of the tin and cool on a wire rack.

To make the frosting, melt the chocolate in a bowl over a saucepan of gently simmering water. Beat the cream cheese and icing sugar together in a second bowl until just mixed. Spoon half into another bowl then stir in the melted chocolate until smooth.

Peel the paper off the cake and cut in half horizontally. Sandwich it back together with the plain frosting and transfer to a plate or tray. Spoon the chocolate frosting over the top and spread into an even layer. Cut into 24 squares, press a candle holder and candle into the centre of each square then decorate with chocolate buttons, sweets and sprinkles. Leave in a cool place for the frosting to firm up.

Tips The cake can be made and decorated the day before then covered with a dome of foil that is tightly sealed around the base of the plate. Keep in the fridge and allow to come to room temperature before serving.

To make the cake more personal, spoon a little melted chocolate into a greaseproof paper piping bag, snip off the tip then pipe initials of the birthday recipient on to a tray lined with non-stick baking paper. Chill until firm then peel off the paper when needed.

Brandy truffles

A box of homemade truffles is always well received and needn't be reserved just for Christmas. Why not take to friends instead of a bottle of wine?

Makes 30
Preparation time:
 1 hour + 5–6 hours
 chilling

150 ml (5 fl oz) **double cream**
200 g (7 oz) **dark chocolate**
 (70% cocoa), broken into pieces
2 tablespoons **icing sugar**
3 tablespoons **brandy**
cocoa powder, for shaping

To decorate

2 tablespoons **cocoa powder**
75 g (2¾ oz) **white chocolate,**
 grated
100 g (3½ oz) **dark chocolate**
 (70% cocoa), broken into pieces
40 g (1½ oz) **milk chocolate**
 (32% cocoa), broken into pieces

Bring the cream just to the boil in a small saucepan, take off the heat and add the chocolate. Leave until melted then add the sugar and gradually stir in the brandy until smooth. Leave to cool then transfer to the fridge for 2–3 hours until firm.

Divide the truffle mixture into 30 mounds on a baking sheet then roll into balls with hands dipped in a little cocoa powder.

Put the 2 tablespoons of cocoa powder on one plate and the grated white chocolate on a second. Roll 10 truffles in cocoa powder and another 10 in the white chocolate then arrange in petit four cases. Put these and the undecorated truffles into the fridge for 2 hours until firm.

Melt the dark chocolate in a bowl set over a saucepan of gently simmering water. Take the undecorated truffles from the fridge and rest one on the tines of a fork held over the melted chocolate. Using a teaspoon, spoon over a little of the chocolate until completely covered. Drain off the excess chocolate then put on a piece of non-stick baking paper. Repeat until all the undecorated truffles are coated. Chill for 10 minutes. Melt the milk chocolate, spoon into a greaseproof piping bag, roll the top down then snip off the tip and pipe a decoration on to each chocolate-covered truffle. Return to the fridge until firm once more then transfer to petit four cases. Arrange in a tissue paper-lined box and tie with ribbon.

Tip If you are feeling adventurous, experiment by bringing the cream just to the boil and flavouring with thyme leaves, a few lavender petals or a little chopped chilli. Leave to stand for the flavours to develop then strain and reheat before adding the chocolate. Alternatively, use a gourmet style bar of ready-flavoured chocolate such as chilli, ginger or lime and add these to the hot cream.

Chocolate cherry cups

These summery petits fours would add a stylish finish to any smart supper or party table.

Makes 18
Preparation time:
 **35 minutes + overnight
 marinating + 2 hours
 chilling**

18 fresh cherries with stalks
2 tablespoons brandy, cherry
 brandy or kirsch
100 g (3½ oz) dark chocolate
 (70% cocoa), broken into pieces
125 ml (4 fl oz) double cream
150 g (5½ oz) white chocolate,
 broken into pieces

Make a slit in the base of each cherry and remove the stone, leaving the stalk still in place. Put the cherries in a small plastic container, add the brandy or liqueur and leave to marinate overnight.

Melt the dark chocolate in a bowl set over a saucepan of simmering water. Put 18 foil petit four cases into the holes in mini muffin tins, or put cases on a small baking tray if you don't have muffin tins.

Spoon a little chocolate into one of the foil cases then brush over the inside of the case with a fine paintbrush. Repeat until all the insides of the cases have been painted. Chill in the fridge for 10 minutes then go back over each case, brushing any thin areas with any remaining chocolate (re-melt the chocolate if necessary). Chill in the fridge until firm.

Meanwhile, bring the cream just to the boil in a small saucepan, add the white chocolate and stir until melted. Chill for 1 hour.

Gradually whisk the brandy or liqueur from the marinated cherries into the chocolate cream until it forms soft swirls, being careful not to over whip. Spoon into a piping bag fitted with a small star nozzle.

Lift the foil cases out of the muffin tins, pipe the white chocolate cream into the cases then top each with a cherry. Chill until ready to serve.

Tip If making these when cherries are out of season, use well-drained canned cherries instead and put these underneath the piped white chocolate cream.